DR. ERNEST DICHTER

STEIN AND DAY/*Publishers*/New York

ACKNOWLEDGMENTS

Many of the concepts that appear in this book have been incorporated into public and corporate in-house developmental seminars conducted by David Nierenberg, Executive Director of Ernest Dichter Associates International. I wish to thank him for his invaluable help.

Mary Solberg has done a wonderful and painstaking job in providing her editorial comments as well as her modern feminine insights. My thanks to her.

First published in 1976
Copyright © 1976 by Ernest Dichter
All rights reserved
Designed by David Miller
Printed in the United States of America
Stein and Day/*Publishers*/Scarborough House, Briarcliff Manor, N.Y. 10510

Library of Congress Cataloging in Publication Data

Dichter, Ernest, 1907-
    Total self-knowledge.

    1. Self-perception—Testing. 2. Projective
techniques. I. Title.
BF697.D53   155.2'84   75-37981
ISBN 0-8128-1919-5

Contents

• 3

Part Three: *How Do You Like Your Work?*

Introduction

Some people say you're high-strung, full of tensions, a bundle of nerves. Others say you're calm, cool, collected.

Which one are you? If you're typical, you have probably never taken the time to add up your assets and deduct from them your liabilities. One of the major human needs is to know oneself better; yet very few tools have been provided to make this kind of self-examination possible on a practical, day-to-day basis. The purpose of this book is to give an introduction to total self-knowledge.

Often we do not realize how we behave. Many people live their whole lives without once looking in the psychological mirror that tells them who they really are. Apparently they are content to live with stereotypes about themselves, like "I'm the way I am, what can I do?" or "I'm just a constant case of nerves." For some, it's as if they had found the ultimate excuse for not doing anything.

The quizzes in this book, while they will tell you a great deal about yourself, are not designed to give you a ready-made blueprint of your personality. As annoying as it might sometimes seem, human beings are flexible, changeable. Because we have a certain amount of elasticity, our lives can be just about as exciting and interesting as we want them to be.

Our personal qualities cover a wide range of possibilities. Whether we stay with what we have, or seek to change some or all of ourselves, is pretty much up to us. Not all of us can become everything we want to be, but fulfilling the potential each of us has is a worthwhile and fascinating adventure. Before we can do it, though, we need to know what we have to work with.

What type of person will get the most out of life? Are you stuck with the "type" you think you are? Or can you change? Some people have tried psychotherapy, but sometimes not even a five-year bout with a psychoanalyst really changes anything. In the end, they may have the same symptoms, although they may simply worry less about them.

The aim of these tests is not for you to pigeonhole or label yourself.

Labels are for museum pieces and cold statues. We hope simply to help you become more aware of yourself, in all areas.

The quizzes that follow are divided into three major categories:

1. *How well do you know yourself?* Instead of simply telling you, "Know thyself," we are trying to help you to gradually understand yourself better, in fact, to help you see yourself as you really are.

2. *How well do you get along with others?* We are not alone in this world. Self-knowledge involves our relationships with others. We may be wonderful, but if we can't get along with others or they can't get along with us, all our great qualities won't help—unless we want to live as hermits.

3. *How do you like your work?* Life can seem purposeless unless we spend time doing something satisfying and worthwhile. Being able to learn, to lead or follow, to organize our time, to evaluate what we do are important elements in an active life.

While we don't claim that these quizzes are foolproof or will give you an ironclad "analysis" of yourself, they should provide several things: first of all, entertainment, and then a guide to appraising honestly what *your* specific strong and weak points are. Whenever possible we have used what are called "projective techniques," techniques that permit us to hide the purpose of each question. Unlike many psychological tests, where the "right" answer is obvious, those in this book are designed in such a way that, whichever answer you choose, it will tell you something new—and possibly important—about yourself, and not just confirm whatever stereotypes you've been carrying around. After all, what fun would it be just to hear and see the same old things again?

While we have tried to avoid making it too obvious what a "good" or "bad" answer would be, you may still have illusions about yourself that don't completely correspond to your real self. Try to be as honest with yourself as you can. Refer as often as possible to your actual behavior or attitudes, not to the kind you think you *should* show or have. If you are asked, for example, whether or not you would ask the waiter to take back food you did not like in a restaurant, do not answer "yes" if, after reflecting, you know you are not very likely to do it.

Perhaps this book should have been called *The Road to Total Self-Knowledge,* for while complete self-knowledge is an ideal, it is the road toward it that is both enjoyable and useful. For instance, if a friend or loved one were to do these quizzes independently and you then compared your copy with his or hers, page by page, you'd be learning about each other as well as about yourself.

The most important thing to be gained from this book is insight into yourself—alone, with others, and in your work. Still, *Total Self-Knowledge* is not a book for self-therapy, but rather a stimulator to action. What will you do with what you find out? We hope the quizzes that follow will help you, challenge you, make you think, but above all encourage you to be the person you want to be.

PART ONE

How Well Do You Know Yourself?

Total self-knowledge begins with *you* . . .

Are You the Person You Really Want to Be?

Can we see ourselves the way we really are? It's difficult—usually because we want to protect ourselves from things we don't want to see. We may feel more secure if we never take a frank look at our personal balance sheet. Or we may check up, find some qualities we admire, but hesitate to make use of them for fear that in the end we will be found wanting. In either case, we're afraid our real self is of little or no value.

The discrepancy between a person's ideal self and his real self usually varies, depending on what qualities we're talking about. What you think of yourself is often more important than what you really are like.

Study the traits below. Check in column 1 the description you think best fits you *as you think you are.* Then check in column 2 the description that best fits *the self you would like to be.*

●

1. *Sense of Humor*

		As you really are	As you'd like to be
a.	Not even a smile.		
b.	Never any laughs.		
c.	Pretty dull.		
d.	At least I can smile.		
e.	Get some laughs.	✗	
f.	Good as most.		✗
g.	Better than my friends.		✓
h.	Joke teller.		
i.	Right up there.	✗	
j.	Like a stand-up comic.		

2. *Poise*

		As you really are	As you'd like to be
a.	A bundle of nerves.	_____	_____
b.	Usually uneasy.	_____	_____
c.	Can't predict.	✕	_____
d.	Need a boost.	_____	_____
e.	Gets me by.	_____	_____
f.	Good as average.	_____	_____
g.	No real qualms.	_____	_____
h.	Only a few doubts.	_____	_____
i.	I even reassure others.	_____	✕
j.	Nothing shakes me.	_____	_____

3. *Intellect*

		As you really are	As you'd like to be
a.	Idiot's delight.	_____	_____
b.	Really a dud.	_____	_____
c.	Just getting by.	_____	_____
d.	Almost average.	_____	_____
e.	Improving daily.	_____	_____
f.	On a par with friends.	_____	_____
g.	Good enough.	_____	_____
h.	Very good.	✕	_____
i.	Bright as a light.	_____	✕
j.	Like a professor.	_____	_____

4. *Psychological temperature.*

		As you really are	As you'd like to be
a.	Cold as Siberia.	_____	_____
b.	Don't like idle contacts.	_____	_____
c.	Can force myself.	_____	_____
d.	Lukewarm. I like distance.	_____	_____
e.	All depends who it is and what for.	✕	_____
f.	I try to be liked.	_____	_____

g. Try to create good "vibes." _____ _____

h. Usually going all out. _____ _____

i. Why not make friends? _____ _____

j. Warm and loving. _____ _____

5. *Appearance*

	As you really are	As you'd like to be
a. Good in the dark.	_____	_____
b. The "before" picture.	_____	_____
c. Nobody sees me.	_____	_____
d. A few admirers.	_____	_____
e. Gaining new admirers.	_____	_____
f. Can compete.	_____	_____
g. I do all right.	_____	_____
h. The mirror smiles back at me.	_____	_____
i. They notice me.	_____	_____
j. Like a movie star.	_____	_____

6. *Charm*

	As you really are	As you'd like to be
a. Like barbed wire.	_____	_____
b. Need to take a course.	_____	_____
c. Rarely shine.	_____	_____
d. I get by.	_____	_____
e. Can force myself.	_____	_____
f. Know how to use it.	_____	_____
g. Some success.	_____	_____
h. A real asset.	_____	_____
i. My long suit.	_____	_____
j. Life of the party.	_____	_____

7. *Adaptability*

	As you really are	As you'd like to be
a. Like a fish out of water.	_____	_____
b. Rarely blend in.	_____	_____
c. Not exactly elastic.	_____	_____

d. It's a strain.   _____   _____
e. Experience helps.   _____   _____
f. Strictly normal.   _____   _____
g. Better than average.   ___×___   _____
h. Handle most cases.   _____   _____
i. Seldom at a loss.   _____   _____
j. Nothing throws me.   _____   ___×___

8. *Consideration for others*

                              As you really are   As you'd like to be

a. I'm No. 1.   _____   _____
b. It's a bother.   ___×___   _____
c. Slips my mind.   _____   _____
d. Always do the right thing.   _____   _____
e. Getting more thoughtful.   _____   _____
f. I do my best.   _____   _____
g. I remember birthdays.   _____   _____
h. A heart of gold.   _____   _____
i. A good deed never hurts.   _____   ___×___
j. Up with the angels.   _____   _____

Please turn the page to find out your score and what it means

SCORING

For all questions:

a = 1	c = 3	e = 5	g = 7	i = 9
b = 2	d = 4	f = 6	h = 8	j = 10

First add the points you checked describing yourself as you think you are. Then add those describing your ideal. Subtract the smaller from the larger number. The difference between the two sums is your score.

A score of less than 20 shows that you are very close to your ideal; see if you think your ideal is too low, or your opinion of yourself is too high. A score of 21 to 40 shows enough margin to keep life interesting; 41 to 60 is average for a person well aware of his faults and eager to improve; 61 to 80 means that you are underestimating yourself or setting your goal too high; anything above 80 means that you are an extreme case; you need to bring your ideals closer to reality.

It is also interesting to check on which traits you are closest to or farthest from your ideal. There are two major categories: *Emotional traits:* 1 (sense of humor), 4 (temperature), 6 (charm), 7 (adaptability). *Intellectual and social traits:* 2 (poise), 3 (intellect), 5 (appearance), and 8 (consideration).

In which one of these two groups are your ideals higher? How close are you to them? If you're pretty far away, how can you start to get closer to reality?

Do You Always Do What You Think You Should Do?

Most of us believe we are decent, law-abiding people. Most of us think we know the difference between right and wrong. But how many of us really behave according to those standards?

Our values are changing. Much of what used to be considered "bad" or "wrong" is no longer quite as shocking as it once was. Often, too, we have the feeling that since some laws, written or unwritten, are themselves wrong, breaking them—or bending them a little—is not so bad, after all.

We have seen enough corruption and lawlessness in places we don't expect to see it—among politicians, doctors, lawyers—so that we wonder, Does anyone really have a sense of values? What ·ever happened to the old-fashioned virtues?

The test that follows will give you some idea of the difference between how "good"—how ethical—you think you are, and how you really act.

Study the situations described below. For each situation, check the choice in column 1 that best describes *how you would really act*. After you have gone through the test once, go back to each situation, and in column 2 check the choice that best describes *how you think you should act* in that situation.

Remember, the test is valuable only if you are completely honest with yourself.

●

1. You go shopping. The cashier gives you the wrong change in your favor.

	HOW I WOULD ACT	HOW I SHOULD ACT
a. I would return the money.	X	X
b. They probably make just as many errors in their favor. I would not return it.		
c. Lucky me! The cashier should have been more careful.	X	

2. You are married to a physician; most of his prescriptions are handled by a particular pharmacy. The pharmacist offers you a discount on merchandise you buy from him.

	HOW I WOULD ACT	HOW I SHOULD ACT
a. It is not quite right, but everybody does it, so why should I not do it?		
b. I would refuse to accept it.		
c. He makes a lot of money through us, so he should give us a discount.	X	X

3. Your spouse's friend invites you to go out.

	HOW I WOULD ACT	HOW I SHOULD ACT
a. It's a free country. Why not take a chance?		
b. I would refuse and say how unfair this is to my spouse.	X	X
c. I would ask permission from my spouse.		

4. You are being paid by the hour. But you often work alone. When you hand in your time sheet, what does it show?

		HOW I WOULD ACT	HOW I SHOULD ACT
a.	An accurate account of the hours.	✗	✗
b.	About 10 percent more than I really worked.		
c.	As many hours as I think I can get away with.	✗	

5. You are having sex with your partner. You are not up to it and do not enjoy it. Would you . . .

		HOW I WOULD ACT	HOW I SHOULD ACT
a.	pretend to reach a climax?	✗	
b.	admit you did not?	✗	✗
c.	admit you didn't only when your partner doubts your statement that you did?		

6. You have a choice between two dates. One is a bore, but knows the best places, is well off, a real swinger, but you really aren't turned on. The second is fascinating but rebellious, has no real plans for the future, little money, but is a good friend and makes you feel comfortable. With whom would you go out?

		HOW I WOULD ACT	HOW I SHOULD ACT
a.	First.		
b.	With both of them alternately.		
c.	Second.	✗	✗

7. I detest my boss. But I need my job. I probably would . . .

		HOW I WOULD ACT	HOW I SHOULD ACT
a.	tell him off and risk losing the job.		
b.	put up with him.	✗	✗
c.	bend over backward to flatter him.		

8. You are working for an advertising agency. You find out that what

they are saying to the public is exaggerated, untrue, or un-necessarily sensational. What action will you take?

		HOW I WOULD ACT	HOW I SHOULD ACT
a.	It's all a game. The people want to be fooled. Why should I care?	_____	_____
b.	I absolutely refuse to work on this assignment.	_____	_____
c.	Realistically, it's my job, after all. But the management should cut down on its unethical behavior, come closer to the truth. At least I will put up a fight.	__X__	__X__

9. You are in a crowded store; it is easy to slip a shirt or a pair of socks into your pocket or briefcase.

		HOW I WOULD ACT	HOW I SHOULD ACT
a.	I have done it or thought about doing it.	__X__	_____
b.	I am too much of a coward; besides, I couldn't bring it off smoothly.	__X__	_____
c.	I could never think about doing such a terrible thing.	_____	_____

10. You had a car accident, but your car also has some damage that dates quite far back and was not covered by insurance.

		HOW I WOULD ACT	HOW I SHOULD ACT
a.	I would not dare claim it, because the insurance company might find out and give me a rough time.	_____	_____
b.	I would try to get the garage to fix both damaged parts and ask them to		

put in a larger bill, including the
previous accident as well.

   c.   It goes against my principles to do
such a thing.

Please turn the page to find out your score and what it means

SCORING

Add your scores for column 1 according to the following key:

1. a = 3	2. a = 1	3. a = 1	4. a = 3	5. a = 1
b = 1	b = 3	b = 3	b = 2	b = 3
c = 2	c = 2	c = 2	c = 1	c = 2
6. a = 1	7. a = 3	8. a = 1	9. a = 1	10. a = 2
b = 2	b = 2	b = 3	b = 2	b = 1
c = 3	c = 1	c = 2	c = 3	c = 3

Now, using the same key, add your scores for column 2. The sum of your scores for column 1 and column 2 is your *total* score.

Each time your "should" score (the way you *should* act) differs from your real behavior, you should subtract a point from your total score.

Your best score would be between 50 and 60, particularly if you got it even after you subtracted your "should" scores from your real ones (first and second columns). You can consider yourself a person with strong principles, pretty honest with yourself, willing to act on your principles.

40-49 suggests that you are accepting the "normal" standards of a civilized society.

28-39 is the "average" score. Most of us are tempted to be somewhat less than "perfect" in our daily behavior. How do you think most people would have scored on this test twenty, thirty, or forty years ago?

20-27 seems almost cynical. Maybe you have a chip on your shoulder; maybe you are convinced that you can make—and break—your own standards.

Are You Basically a Happy Person?

Happiness is a common yardstick for measuring our success in living. To five-year-olds, happiness is an affectionate hug or a chunk carved out of the Chippendale table. To adults, whose needs are more complex, it may be absorbing work or the security of a good marriage.

To the poet Robert Burns, happiness was "just a word," with a different meaning for each individual. Whatever the recipe, it remains an emotion of the heart, an inner contentment felt when some basic need or desire is realized.

Happiness is often *a way of looking at life.* Happy people usually have a zest for living. They enjoy the little things as well as the big ones. They have an attitude of anticipation; they expect life to be exciting—or at least interesting.

To test your happiness quotient, picture each "slice of life" described below. Then, for each, check the *one* caption that best describes how you react to what you see. You'll be surprised by what your reactions to these situations tell you about your own capacity for happiness!

•

2
2
2
1
1
3
2
2
2
1

1. A chemist standing in a laboratory, measuring a formula.

   ☒ a. That kind of work requires great precision.
   ☐ b. Absorbed in the work and loves it.
   ☐ c. Thinks the job is necessary, but dull.

2. A picnic around a campfire; everybody is busy helping out.

   ☒ a. Get-togethers with friends are a lot of fun.
   ☐ b. That kind of thing doesn't appeal to me.
   ☐ c. They're enjoying each other's company; isn't that the most important thing?

3. Mother and father sitting in their living room, reading to their children.

   - ☑ a. What a beautiful family!
   - ☒ b. I'm sure they have their problems, but I'd bet they manage to solve them.
   - ☐ c. Another dull evening at home with the kids.

4. College graduation.

   - ☐ a. What a thrill!
   - ☐ b. It's a silly nuisance, all this ceremony.
   - ☒ c. It's fine, if it doesn't take too long.

5. A woman picking a tomato in her backyard garden.

   - ☐ a. It sure took long enough!
   - ☒ b. I *did* it! My very own tomatoes!
   - ☐ c. Was all that work really worth it?

6. Man shows his wife the check he's just written. It's the last payment on the mortgage.

   - ☒ a. It took a long time, but we made it. The house is *ours*.
   - ☐ b. Well, that's one less debt. Let's see how long it will take to get rid of the others.
   - ☐ c. Twenty years, and what have we got? The house already needs another new coat of paint.

7. Boy hands his parents a present, bought with his first earnings.

   - ☒ a. It's great to be able to give *them* something for a change.
   - ☐ b. That's all I can afford. I hope they won't hold it against me.
   - ☐ c. I wonder if they're thinking, It's about time!

24 •

8. Woman walking out of a hospital, saying goodbye to the nurses.

- [ ] a. I thought I'd never get out of here alive. Am I glad!
- [x] b. I don't believe that bill! Still, it's only money and after all, I am as good as new again.
- [ ] c. What a miserable place! I hope I'll never have to go back there again.

Please turn the page to find out your score and what it means

SCORING

Check your answers with the table below. Then add up your points for total score.

1. a = 2	2. a = 3	3. a = 3	4. a = 3
b = 3	b = 1	b = 2	b = 1
c = 1	c = 2	c = 1	c = 2
5. a = 1	6. a = 3	7. a = 3	8. a = 2
b = 3	b = 2	b = 2	b = 3
c = 2	c = 1	c = 1	c = 1

A score between 18 and 24 shows that you get much pleasure and satisfaction from life; 13 to 17 indicates that you have ups and downs; if your score is 11 or 12, or even lower, ask yourself whether you don't look for the shadow instead of the sun too often.

Are You Realistic?

Many of us are tempted, when things get tough, to become "make-believe" artists. "Yes, but" may be our favorite phrase. It is good to be optimistic, but kidding ourselves instead of taking action and correcting a situation that needs it can be dangerous.

To see how well you face reality, check the one statement in each pair below that agrees with your views.

●

1. ☐ a. One day I shall be rich and famous.
    ☒ b. It won't happen just thinking about it. There must be a plan.

2. ☐ a. It is entirely possible for two people to fall in love at first sight.
    ☒ b. It is necessary for two people to know each other well to really fall in love.

3. ☐ a. Most people worry needlessly. Things usually work out all right.
    ☒ b. Life is full of problems. You never know what's going to happen next.

4. ☒ a. It's wise to put your fears out of your mind until you have to face them.
    ☐ b. The only way to eliminate fear is to face it squarely and remove its causes.

5. ☐ a. People are intelligent enough to guarantee good government.
    ☒ b. Unless they watch out, people can easily be misled.

6. ☒ a. A vivid imagination is a genuine asset to the person who has one.

   ☐ b. Too much imagination can be dangerous.

7. ☐ a. When things go wrong, I take comfort in the saying "Every cloud has a silver lining."

   ☒ b. Things will be bad till I make them better.

8. ☐ a. Mankind has always found a solution. We will make progress.

   ☒ b. There is no guarantee that the world as we know it will survive.

Please turn the page to find out your score and what it means

SCORING

Every *a* statement checked receives a score of five, and every *b* statement receives a score of zero.

A total score of around 40 indicates that you prefer a world *you* have created, rather than the real one. Near zero means you have your feet on the ground—if not in a rut. Most people score around 20. *10*

People have a right to their dreams, to feel powerful enough to change the world. But too often these same people, when confronted with the "cold, cruel world," move to the other extreme and refuse to believe in any dream.

We need a combination of both: realism and hope.

Often two people are attracted to each other because one is the realist and the other the dreamer. If your partner has a copy of this book, compare your responses and see if it's true that "opposites attract."

How Down-to-Earth Are You?

All of us are escapists to some degree. We live in the city and dream of a peaceful chicken farm. (We are deliberately unrealistic, so we don't think about feed prices and poultry diseases.) Or we farm for a living and dream of an easy job which we can leave at 5 P.M., which would allow us to enjoy our weekends and receive a paycheck with delightful regularity. (We do not consider the supervisor's temper or the dissatisfaction of seeing only a part of the product of our work.) Or we have a cocktail, and then settle down with a light novel.

Such occasional indulgences are normal, useful safety valves for letting off steam. Complete lack of self-indulgence is just as undesirable as a strong tendency to run away and shirk responsibilities.

Picture the six situations described below. Then check the *one* caption for each picture that best expresses your interpretation.

●

1. Man on a deserted beach on a tropical island.

    ☐ a. That's the life. I wish I could be in his place.
    ☒ b. A great place to visit, but I wouldn't want to live there.
    ☐ c. Wherever you go, you take your problems with you.
    ☐ d. I wonder when he will have had enough.

2. Woman sitting in bed reading a book. The book is . . .

    ☐ a. a report she must analyze for tomorrow's business conference.
    ☐ b. the latest on the international situation.
    ☒ c. a detective or mystery story.
    ☐ d. about life in a commune.

3. You won $50,000 in prizes as a contestant in a TV show. What is your immediate reaction?

- ☐ a. I am not going to change my life very much. I would keep on working, maybe pay off some debts.
- ☐ b. I would take a long vacation, really have a ball. It will last as long as it does.
- ☒ c. I would enjoy myself, but also invest most of the money for later time.
- ☐ d. Taxes would eat up most of it, even if I were lucky enough to win such a prize, which I doubt.

4. Sign painter printing PRESIDENT on an office door. He thinks . . .

- ☐ a. "I'm in a rut. I should change jobs."
- ☐ b. "I'll go to night school, train for another job. Then I'll have a private office, too."
- ☒ c. "Someday I'll be president of my own company."
- ☒ d. "I was never cut out to be president of anything."

5. You pass a betting window at a race track. You think . . .

- ☐ a. "With some luck, I could make a lot of money here."
- ☒ b. "This is a good way to take your mind off things."
- ☐ c. "In the long run, you can't beat the races."
- ☒ d. "I'll only make it by working hard at my own job."

6. Man sitting at a desk behind a heap of papers. He thinks . . .

- ☐ a. "Things just seem to pile up. I wonder when the ax is going to fall."
- ☒ b. "I'll just do one thing at a time."
- ☐ c. "I've got too much on my mind right now. I'll tackle these papers tomorrow."
- ☐ d. "Maybe Mr. Jones will forget he wrote, if I just let his letter go for another week."

SCORING

Check your answers and add them according to the following key:

1. a = 4	2. a = 2	3. a = 2
b = 3	b = 1	b = 4
c = 1	c = 3	c = 3
d = 2	d = 4	d = 1

4. a = 3	5. a = 4	6. a = 3
b = 2	b = 3	b = 1
c = 4	c = 2	c = 2
d = 1	d = 1	d = 4

17-24: A nonchalant attitude combined with a belief that things somehow will take care of themselves.

10-16: The "average" escapist.

6-9: You may want to escape more often; you use "controlled escapism."

Set a limit, but get out from under every so often. It is good relaxation.

Do You Show Your Feelings or Conceal Them?

Some of us seem inscrutable. No one else can decipher our real feelings. Others of us can be read like a book. Every little disappointment or worry is registered in our behavior, the way we react, talk, and use our body.

Showing one's feelings—or not showing them—is a pattern developed in our youth, copied from our parents, or learned from friends and associates, and it is admittedly difficult to modify this pattern.

Such new psychotherapeutic schools as "assertiveness training" contend that you should always express your feelings. Other people advise you that "he who speaks in anger is a fool." Much depends on the situation and your temperament.

Sometimes it is helpful to be demonstrative and at other times it helps to hide one's feelings.

We think it might be interesting for you to test yourself to find out what your most frequent behavior is. For each of the following situations, which answer appeals to you most or corresponds to what you think your behavior usually is? Be honest, please!

●

1. You are seeing a very sentimental and gripping movie or TV show.

   ☑ a. I cry quite easily.
   ☐ b. It's just a play; I stay calm.
   ☐ c. Even if I am touched, I hide my feelings.

2. You are late for a party you have been invited to.

   ☑ a. I seek out the hostess right away and apologize.
   ☐ b. I wait till an opportunity arises to make amends.
   ☑ c. I don't do anything to excuse myself for being late.

3. Something important—good or bad or exciting—happens to you.

  ☐ a. I reflect on it by myself.
  ☒ b. I discuss it with close friends or family.
  ☒ c. I call as many of my friends or acquaintances as I can to discuss the event with them.

4. You had a fight with a member of your family or a colleague.

  ☒ a. I tend to shout or to argue.
  ☐ b. I walk out quietly.
  ☐ c. I make my point and terminate the discussion.

5. You are being criticized, partially for just and partially for unjust reasons.

  ☐ a. I agree with the critic and try to correct my mistakes.
  ☐ b. I defend myself and decide to get back at the detractor in one way or another.
  ☒ c. I try to explain to the critic why I did what I did.

6. You see a newlywed couple embracing each other passionately.

  ☒ a. I am embarrassed and turn away.
  ☐ b. Why don't they wait until they are alone?
  ☒ c. I might do the same thing.

7. You are in physical pain. A friend appears.

  ☒ a. I whimper loud enough for him or her to hear it.
  ☐ b. I groan and swear.
  ☐ c. I stay quiet and try to hide my misery.

8. Someone tells a joke that I think is in poor taste.

  ☐ a. I tell him or her off in no uncertain terms.
  ☒ b. I pretend not to have heard it.
  ☐ c. I frown, but say nothing.

Please turn the page to find out your score and what it means

SCORING

Add up the numbers corresponding to the letters you checked for each question:

1. a = 3 b = 2 c = 1	2. a = 3 b = 2 c = 1	3. a = 1 b = 2 c = 3	4. a = 3 b = 1 c = 2
5. a = 1 b = 3 c = 2	6. a = 2 b = 1 c = 3	7. a = 2 b = 3 c = 1	8. a = 3 b = 1 c = 2

If you feel like letting everything out, it is usually better for your type to do so, for if you suppress your anger or annoyance, it may make itself felt somewhere else by somebody who may be quite innocent.

20-24: You are more likely to let your feelings show, and should accent this pattern.

13-19: You use judgment and are outspoken or not, depending on the situation. (This score would apply to most people.)

8-12: You have either a very quiet nature or a tendency to suppress your feelings. You might try to let yourself go in certain situations and experience the relief of getting mad once in a while, or expressing joy and pleasure in an uninhibited way.

Do Your Nerves Get the Best of You?

Some of us consider ourselves cool as cucumbers. Others are convinced that a state of nervous tension is usual.

The threshold of irritability varies with most of us. If too many challenges stream in on us, most of us will overreact. We feel we can't take it. With some people it takes relatively little to produce such excitement: others seem not to be affected no matter how much turmoil swirls around them.

Think of the most upsetting experience you ever had—perhaps you were falsely arrested. That is 10 on your anxiety scale. Then think of a time you weren't at all anxious. That is zero. Now, imagine yourself in the following situations and rate yourself from zero to ten in the spaces next to the questions.

●

_____ 1. Your child is ill with the measles, and is running a high fever.

_____ 2. You are caught in an elevator between floors for three hours.

_____ 3. You are about to have an interview for a job you've always wanted.

_____ 4. While driving through a strange city, you lose your way.

_____ 5. You have to wait in line to buy your airplane ticket; the P.A. system announces your flight.

_____ 6. You are taking a bath when the doorbell rings.

_____ 7. You are several blocks from home, and it begins to rain cats and dogs.

_____ 8. You are making love and the phone rings.

_____ 9. The dentist is running behind schedule, and you have to wait in his office.

_____ 10. You are sitting home one night; lightning flashes, and suddenly all the lights go out.

_____ 11. You are riding with a friend who is driving much too fast.

_____ 12. While cleaning up in the kitchen, you gash your finger on a broken glass.

Around 60 - Average ; Sometime excitable/cool
Approaches 120 - Nervous Wreck
Around 0 - Reckless, watch for danger

SCORING

How anxious are you? Simply add the scores you gave yourself on the 12 questions. If your total approaches 120, you're probably a nervous wreck. If it's around 0, you may be reckless, and may blunder into real danger. If your score is around 60, you are like most of us, sometimes excitable, sometimes cool and collected.

Are nerves a problem for you? If so, it may be that you aren't afraid of the immediate situation; you fear what may grow out of it. You expect the worst. Remember, a little nervousness may be helpful, may warn you of danger ahead. Calmly study each upsetting experience. Don't waste your energy in useless anxiety. A sense of humor will help, too, by putting your fears in perspective.

How Adaptable Are You?

Someone once said the only thing we can really count on is change. How well you handle changes will determine how well you live. If you adapt yourself to meet the difficulties that arise from day to day, this should help you meet major changes, too.

A business opportunity, an injury, a loss—or sudden good fortune— represents a challenge that calls for a new way of doing things. How well you adapt tests your resourcefulness, intelligence, and courage.

Put yourself in the following situations. Then select the alternative you think best describes what you would do.

•

1. You come home very late. All the doors are locked, and everyone is asleep. You have no key. What will you do?

    ☐ a. Throw pebbles at one of the windows, probably the bedroom.
    ☐ b. Try to jimmy open a window or door.
    ☒ c. Go to a nearby phone and call the people in the house.

2. On your way to give a lecture or meet important people, you discover you forgot to put on your cufflinks. Can you think of a quick simple solution?

    ☐ a. Use paper clips.
    ☒ b. Make a joke about it.
    ☒ c. Roll up your sleeves.

3. You forget to take your medicine every four hours as the doctor told you to. What can you do to remind yourself?

    ☒ a. Set an alarm clock.
    ☒ b. Write a note and put it up on the wall.
    ☐ c. Mark four-hour intervals on an easily visible clock.

4. You have found a special picnic spot in the woods. You would like to hike a little longer, but still be able to get back to it easily. What method could you use?

    ☒ a. Break the twigs on the trees leading to the picnic spot.
    ☐ b. Build a fire you know will smoke a lot.
    ☒ c. Mark the trail with pebbles as you walk away.

5. You must undergo a serious operation that may change your life. What are you most likely to ask your doctor?

    ☒ a. What will I still be able to do after the operation?
    ☐ b. Can I get another opinion?
    ☐ c. Should I or can I retire completely after the operation?

6. You are about to be transferred to a foreign country. You are not familiar with either the language or the customs. What are you most likely to do in preparation for your trip?

    ☐ a. Find out whether other Americans live there and how you can contact them.
    ☒ b. Take a crash course on the language and customs of the country.
    ☒ c. Try to meet some natives of the country before you leave.

7. You have lost your job. There are very few openings in your field. What are you most likely to do?

    ☐ a. Apply for unemployment compensation, and hope.
    ☐ b. Write to various companies that might have openings in your field.
    ☒ c. Find out which of your skills can be applied to other fields.

8. You have an urgent appointment some blocks away. A severe storm has made the streets almost impassable. What will you do?

    ☐ a. Wait till the water recedes.
    ☐ b. Take off your shoes and stockings and walk.
    ☒ c. Postpone the appointment.

Please turn the page to find out your score and what it means

SCORING

Add up your scores on the quiz according to the following key:

1. a = 3 b = 1 c = 2	2. a = 3 b = 2 c = 1	3. a = 2 b = 1 c = 3	4. a = 3 b = 2 c = 1
5. a = 3 b = 2 c = 1	6. a = 1 b = 2 c = 3	7. a = 1 b = 2 c = 3	8. a = 1 b = 3 c = 2

If your score is between 18 and 24, you are resourceful and can think of creative solutions to various problems. A score of 13 to 17 puts you in the category of the average person, who sometimes welcomes, sometimes avoids, challenges presented by a change. 8-12 may indicate that you need to learn to welcome change and consider it a challenge rather than a threat.

Every day we are forced to practice adaptability, if only to get up from an easy chair and be hospitable to visitors. We can accustom ourselves to change by deliberately seeking new experiences. When we do learn to adapt, we often discover hidden resources for meeting many problems we never thought we could face.

How Well Do You Handle a Crisis?

You've suddenly lost your job. The world seems to be collapsing around you. You're ready to give up. You would like to run away—forget it all—or have somebody appear like a fairy godmother and pull you out of all this trouble.

Deep down, however, you know it's all up to you. No one can really help you unless you are ready to help yourself.

The following questions will increase your insight about how well you can take it.

●

1. Because you just missed your train, you have to rearrange your trip. What is your most likely reaction?

   ☒ a. I am furious about it all day.
   ☒ b. I am annoyed, but try to make different arrangements. Next time, I'll try to avoid operating on such a tight schedule.
   ☐ c. Of course I am not happy, but I usually try to make the best of it on the spot.

2. Everything seems to happen at the same time. The phone rings, there's a knock at the door, and you have to finish fixing supper. What is your reaction likely to be?

   ☐ a. I can't do it all at once. I want to drop everything and walk out.
   ☒ b. I concentrate on priorities and put unimportant things aside.
   ☒ c. I stay calm, speed up my work tempo, and, most of the time, get everything done.

3. You lost a lot of money all at once (either through foolish speculation or because you got caught in a swindle). What is your most likely reaction?

☒ a. I blame myself or somebody else and really suffer.

☐ b. I tell myself I can't always be right and think of ways of making it up some other way.

☐ c. I cut my losses and forget about them fairly soon.

4. Your mate (boyfriend or girlfriend, husband or wife) told you he/she was leaving you. You are just not compatible and he/she has found somebody else. Which reaction comes closest to your own?

☒ a. We were never suited to each other anyway; he/she had the courage to admit it.

☐ b. I must have done something wrong. I should have tried harder to understand him/her. It was all my fault.

☐ c. No one could have lived with him/her. He/she is impossible. At least I didn't have to be the one to break up the relationship.

5. You have just been fired. Your employer gave inadequate work as an excuse, but you're not sure whether it was your lack of ability or simply not having been given enough chance. Which of the following reactions is closest to your own?

☐ a. Plead with the employer to give you another chance.

☒ b. Being fired is proof of another failure; next time I'll end up the same way.

☒ c. From now on I'll have to fight for my success.

6. You have to relocate at the request of your company. Your wife and/or your family is very upset. How do you think you would handle such a crisis?

☐ a. I am the breadwinner. I can't let such an opportunity go by. We'll move. Period.

☑ b. I'll get as much information about the new location as I can and try to convince my family how nice the move will be.

☐ c. I won't sacrifice the happiness of my family. I will tell my company I can't move. Either they will accept my decision or I shall look for another job.

Please turn the page to find out your score and what it means

SCORING

Add up your scores based on the following key:

1. a = 1	2. a = 1	3. a = 1
b = 2	b = 2	b = 2
c = 3	c = 3	c = 3

4. a = 3	5. a = 1	6. a = 2
b = 2	b = 2	b = 3
c = 1	c = 3	c = 1

A score of 15 to 18 shows that you can handle a crisis very well. 10-14 indicates that you can take it most of the time. 6-9 could mean that it would be a good idea for you to learn to accept life on its own terms and to roll more with the punches.

In crisis, a well-established pattern or system suddenly breaks down. It is as if an apparently well-built house collapses. The best way to build it up again is to remove the debris, clean up, sort out, and organize. The same thing applies to our everyday life. Looking back, moaning about what you have lost, helps little. You can learn something from the way you handle almost any kind of crisis.

How Uninhibited Are You?

Suggest skinny-dipping in mixed company and you will discover quickly who is and who is not inhibited.

Some people seem to open up easily and talk about anything without hesitating. Others want to disappear when they are asked to approach someone and ask a favor.

Being too shy to get up and speak in public or too inhibited to take off your jacket at a meeting because no one else does can be due to fear of ridicule and can hamper you in many ways. We all carry in our subconscious minds a number of similar forgotten warnings, commands, and "don'ts." We have not only forgotten where these rules came from; we often don't even realize that they exist.

How inhibited are you really? The following test may give you some insight:

●

1. You see an old friend across the street. What would you do?

    ☒ a. Call out to him, even though many people would turn their heads.

    ☐ b. Run across the street to say hello.

    ☒ c. Wave and hope that he will see you.

2. You discover that you have a grease stain on your shirt or blouse. You have to go to an important meeting. What do you do?

    ☒ a. Say nothing.

    ☐ b. Make a joke about the spot.

    ☐ c. Try to cover it up or even skip the meeting.

3. You are invited to go skinny-dipping at a party. Would you . . .

    ☐ a. get undressed right away and dive in?

    ☒ b. wait till the others get undressed?

    ☒ c. refuse to participate?

4. On your way to meet a friend, you have a flat tire, which you wind up changing yourself. You're dirty and disheveled afterward. What would you do next?

    ☒ a. Hesitate but meet your friend anyway.
    ☐ b. Feel reasonably comfortable about it.
    ☐ c. Get washed up first and keep the friend waiting.

5. You happen to come upon the scene of an accident that has just happened. The victim is lying on the ground, bloody. If the ambulance attendant asked you to help him, would you . . .

    ☐ a. refuse?
    ☐ b. apologize and find an excuse?
    ☒ c. be eager to help?

6. While walking through a park, you suddenly come upon a couple lying on the grass, making love. Would you . . .

    ☐ a. watch from behind a tree?
    ☒ b. turn away in embarrassment?
    ☐ c. watch openly, if they don't mind?

Please turn the page to find out your score and what it means

SCORING

Score yourself according to the following key:

1. a = 3	2. a = 3	3. a = 3
b = 2	b = 2	b = 2
c = 1	c = 1	c = 1

4. a = 2	5. a = 1	6. a = 2
b = 3	b = 2	b = 1
c = 1	c = 3	c = 3

The higher your score the less inhibited you are. 18-16 shows that you apply few brakes, have few inhibitions. 6-9 indicates that you are quite inhibited. The question you must ask yourself is: Do my inhibitions keep me from doing what I want to do? If the answer is yes, you might spend some time investigating where they come from and what you can do about overcoming them.

A score of 10-15 puts you among the majority of people, who do not remove the brake entirely. We do need some controls to live happily in a social world, after all.

Do You Think You Worry Too Much?

"I wonder what my boss will say when he finds out I forgot to call and cancel that appointment?"

"I wonder what Mother will say if I tell her we're not coming to dinner Sunday!"

"I'm worried about her. She's not usually late."

Sound like anyone you know?

Worrying is usually a matter of fear—being afraid of "what *might* happen if . . ." Often, too, worrying is a great substitute for doing something about a situation or problem that needs action. We convince ourselves that nothing can be done, and to pay for not doing anything, we worry.

How much of a worrier are you? The following test may tell you a great deal about yourself. Read the phrase beside each number below and check the answer that most accurately describes just how often you worry about the situation the phrase brings to mind.

●

1. Being out of work
   - ☒ a. Very frequently
   - ☐ b. Often
   - ☒ c. Occasionally
   - ☐ d. Never

2. Having a car accident
   - ☐ a. Very frequently
   - ☐ b. Often
   - ☒ c. Occasionally
   - ☐ d. Never

3. Being sick
   - ☐ a. Very frequently
   - ☐ b. Often
   - ☒ c. Occasionally
   - ☐ d. Never

4. Owing money
   - ☐ a. Very frequently
   - ☐ b. Often
   - ☒ c. Occasionally
   - ☐ d. Never

5. Being mugged or robbed
   - ☐ a. Very frequently
   - ☒ b. Often
   - ☐ c. Occasionally
   - ☒ d. Never

6. Dying
   - ☒ a. Very frequently
   - ☐ b. Often
   - ☒ c. Occasionally
   - ☐ d. Never

7. Growing old
   - ☐ a. Very frequently
   - ☐ b. Often
   - ☒ c. Occasionally
   - ☐ d. Never

8. Being alone
   - ☒ a. Very frequently
   - ☒ b. Often
   - ☐ c. Occasionally
   - ☐ d. Never

Please turn the page to find out your score and what it means

SCORING

Score 3 for each time you answered "very frequently," 2 for "often," 1 for "occasionally," and 0 for "never."

If your total score for eight categories is 3 or less, you are confident and carefree, perhaps even happy-go-lucky. A score of 4 or 5 indicates that you are a "healthy" worrier; you think about the future, but you are not too concerned about it. The average person will score 6, 7, or 8. A total score of 9 or more indicates that you may have a tendency to create imaginary obstacles and worry unnecessarily.

One way of combatting worry is to concentrate on what is happening *now*, while it is happening. There are many things you should have done differently and there will be many wrong decisions you will make in the future, but right now—today—you can do at least a few things and do them right. You can try to make the most of the present moment. By making good use of the possibilities of the present, you will build up a reserve of experiences which, when past, will no longer worry you. Your energy will be focused on immediate opportunities, and you'll let the future take care of itself.

Do You Feel Guilty More Often Than Other People?

All of us feel guilty about some things: thoughts, feelings, and acts. Somewhere along the way we have learned what is "good" and what is "bad," and we have also learned that if we do what is "bad," we will be punished. If there is no one else around to punish us for being "bad," we tend to do it ourselves by feeling guilty.

What's really important is to discover what we feel guilty about—and what we do with those guilt feelings. Do we punish ourselves over and over again? Do we take those guilt feelings out on those around us? Do we forgive ourselves?

To see what you feel guilty about, look at the quiz below. Put yourself in the situation described, then check the answer that best approximates your own response:

●

1. You've just sent in your income-tax form. You did a little cheating here and there. How do you feel about it?

   ☑ a. I never give it a second thought.
   ☐ b. Everyone tells a few lies, cheats a little. Why shouldn't I?
   ☐ c. I shouldn't have lied on the form.

2. You've had a few too many at a party. Suddenly you hear yourself saying, "I've been in this business longer than anyone here, and let me tell you, I know what works and what doesn't. Your idea won't." After the party, you remember what you said. How do you feel now?

   ☐ a. What a rotten thing for me to say! I really came off as a know-it-all!
   ☑ b. Well, I do know this business better than anyone else.
   ☐ c. I hope no one remembers how arrogant I sounded.

3. You don't feel like working. You are just fed up. You call the office and tell them that you sprained your ankle and you'll be out for a few days. It is a lie. How do you feel about it?

- ☑ a. I am sure everyone in our office has used such excuses. The only difference is the ingenuity of the excuse.
- ☐ b. I would much rather tell them I was tired or feeling blah and would not accomplish much. I would promise to make it up some other time.
- ☐ c. I would suffer more from my guilt feelings than staying home from work would be worth.

4. You yelled at your spouse, although he or she was not really at fault. You were upset and just took it out on him or her. How do you feel about it afterward?

- ☑ a. I would apologize and go out of my way to be nice.
- ☑ b. I would explain my reaction and talk it out.
- ☐ c. I have a right to get mad once in a while; my spouse has to understand that.

5. You just feel like splurging. You go to an expensive restaurant by yourself and order what you like, regardless of price. When you see the bill, what is your reaction?

- ☐ a. What a stupid thing to do! I could have used the money to buy something nice for myself or for my family.
- ☑ b. I deserve a treat once in a while. I skimp often enough.
- ☐ c. I really went overboard. A few good dishes would have been enough. There was no need to order the most expensive things.

6. You have a chance to take an item from a store shelf without too much risk of getting caught. There is no one around. You slide it quickly into your pocket. What is your feeling?

58 •

☐ a. I did it. I saved a couple of dollars.

☒ b. I really should not have done it. Suppose I had been caught! Imagine the embarrassment and trouble!

☐ c. I just would not do it, no matter how great the temptation.

Please turn the page to find out your score and what it means

SCORING

Add up your score according to the following key:

1. a = 1
  b = 2
  c = 3
	2. a = 3
	  b = 1
	  c = 2
		3. a = 1
		  b = 2
		  c = 3

4. a = 3
  b = 2
  c = 1
	5. a = 3
	  b = 1
	  c = 2
		6. a = 1
		  b = 2
		  c = 3

The higher your score, the more often you feel guilty. If you scored between 18 and 14, you are a real puritan. Either you feel we should be saints or you have a rare and genuine sense of morality, which you never deviate from.

A score of 9 to 13 is more realistic. Most of us do lie or cheat to some extent, feel guilty about doing so, but can also rationalize these things.

A score of 6 to 8 indicates a very low degree of guilt feelings. Perhaps your values are freer and more tolerant than most people's, or perhaps you feel we should make decisions without too many regrets afterward.

Are You a Hypochondriac?

We all know how boring it is to sit at the phone for hours while someone—a friend or relative, usually—tells us about each new ache and pain he or she has discovered since the last time we talked. This kind of monologue makes most of us wish we had never asked, "How are you?"

But which of us has never made a big deal out of a headache when we wanted some sympathy? Which of us has never developed a stomach ache when, as children, we didn't want to go to school one morning?

There's a little of the hypochondriac in all of us. Having something physical to complain about can be an attention getter, when other means seem less effective. What's important is how much we depend on this method, how often we use it, and whether we really begin to believe our own complaints, even when it's obvious that they are mostly in our minds.

How much of a hypochondriac are you? The following test may tell you some interesting things about yourself. Check the letter of the answer that best describes your reaction.

●

1. • A sore that does not heal, particularly in the mouth.
   • A painless lump, especially in the breast, lip, or tongue.
   • Irregular bleeding from any of the natural body openings.
   • Progressive change in the color or size of wart, mole, or birthmark.
   • Persistent indigestion.
   • Continued hoarseness, unexplained cough, or difficulty in swallowing.
   • Any change in bowel habits.

   The above list contains seven warning signs of cancer. Did you:
   - ☐ a. Glance at them casually, then go on?
   - ☑ b. Check to see which ones applied to you?
   - ☐ c. Read it with an eye for information?

2. Two equally good doctors have interpreted your symptoms differently based on the same tests. One is convinced that you have a tumor, the other tells you that nothing could be found and all the evidence is negative. Your reaction?

☐ a. I am inclined to accept the opinion of the doctor who is reassuring.

☐ b. I am more ready to believe that the more pessimistic doctor may be right and that there is something there after all.

☐ c. I would consult a third doctor and then accept the majority opinion.

3. You are not feeling very well. You have a headache and feel tired. What are you most likely to do?

☐ a. Take an aspirin and lie down for a while.

☐ b. Call the doctor and make an appointment.

☐ c. Keep on working and hope that the symptoms will go away by themselves.

4. You hear about a friend's illness. He/She is not quite sure what it is. You are being asked to come for a visit. What would you do?

☐ a. Wait till I am sure what he/she suffers from, to make sure it is not contagious.

☐ b. Ask the friend what the symptoms are and whether a doctor had seen him/her, and then decide whether to visit her/him or not.

☐ c. Rush over and find out whether you can be of help.

5. You don't feel up to par and would like to stay home from work. What, as far as you remember honestly, is your most likely reaction?

☐ a. I call up the work place and tell them I feel tired and stay home.

☐ b. I look for symptoms, such as a sniffle or "funny feeling," then I feel better because I found a more reasonable-sounding story as an explanation.

    ☐   c. I force myself to go to work; I feel the "blah" feeling will go away and it usually does.

6. On TV there is a filmed report of an operation on a brain tumor. What are you likely to do?

    ☐   a. Stay glued to the screen and watch every detail.
    ☐   b. Turn the set off or turn to a different program.
    ☐   c. It is more interesting than a who-done-it show. You identify with the doctors.

Please turn the page to find out your score and what it means

SCORING

Add your scores according to the following key:

1. a = 1	2. a = 1	3. a = 2
b = 3	b = 3	b = 3
c = 2	c = 2	c = 1
4. a = 3	5. a = 2	6. a = 2
b = 2	b = 3	b = 3
c = 1	c = 1	c = 1

If your total score is 6-8, you are very sensible about your body and your concerns with yourself. 9-15 makes you a member of the broad "middle class" of hypochondriacs. You try whenever you can get away with it to get sympathy either for yourself or others. A high score of 16-18 indicates that you ought to work on a change of attitude. Chances are you don't need to be sick to be an interesting person others will pay attention to. Try it; you may surprise yourself.

How Well Do You Handle Frustrations?

Remember the last time you had an appointment with someone who kept you waiting? First you watched the crowd, thought about other things. As the minutes passed you became impatient, couldn't stand still. When your friend finally arrived, you snapped at him without waiting to hear why he was late. Your crossness with your friend is a typical example of frustrated behavior.

It is the same feeling that makes you bark at your spouse when the boss has criticized your work and hurt your feelings. The boss isn't available, or you are afraid to talk back to him, so you let off steam on whoever happens to be around.

Sometimes frustration shows itself in still another way: you get angry at yourself and look for something—food or drink—to compensate for what you feel you have missed.

All of us are frustrated to a certain extent. It is only when we do not recognize frustration and its effects that it becomes dangerous and threatens to get out of control.

The following test may tell you something about how well you handle frustrations. Check the letter next to the response that comes closest to your own.

●

1. You have been expecting a check in the mail for the last few weeks. You open the mail. Nothing. What are you most likely to do?

   ☒ a. Call the party and blow up on the phone.
   ☐ b. Set a time limit. I'll wait three more days, but then . . .
   ☐ c. Do nothing but wait.

2. You just had your car fixed, to the tune of $150. It breaks down again.

    ☒ a. Get mad at the mechanic or repair shop and give them hell.

    ☐ b. Check everything out first to see whether it is not your fault.

    ☐ c. Deliberately smash something else and blame the mechanic.

3. You bought an article of clothing for someone as a birthday present. It does not fit.

    ☒ a. I'll send it back despite the trouble.

    ☐ b. I'll wait till I can give it to somebody else.

    ☐ c. I'll try to get it fitted if it is possible.

4. You have written a very complicated letter explaining a problem to a friend. When you are about to mail it you can't find it anywhere. What is your most likely reaction?

    ☐ a. Maybe it is better this way. I won't write it again. It is too much trouble.

    ☒ b. I'll rewrite it. It will be more concise and better thought through this time, anyway.

    ☐ c. I'll keep on looking; maybe I can find it after all. In the meantime I shall send a very short note to my friend, without bothering with all the details.

5. You signed a paper or a contract without having read it properly and you discover that you have been had.

    ☒ a. I call up the district attorney or any other public agency to file a complaint.

    ☐ b. I get mad at myself for having been so stupid and decide I'll get even with someone else if I can't reach this guy.

    ☐ c. I learned my lesson. I swallow my pride and don't tell anybody about it.

6. You think you have done a good job, but instead of giving you compliments for it, the people you work for pick on minor points.

☐ a. I will make the corrections they want. No sense arguing with people who don't really understand, anyway.

☒ b. I refuse to have my work changed. That destroys its basic value and my own approach.

☐ c. I will argue with them and try to explain what I intended to do and see whether I can't get them to accept part of my views.

Please turn the page to find out your score and what it means

SCORING

Add your score according to the following key:

1. a = 3	2. a = 2	3. a = 3
b = 2	b = 1	b = 2
c = 1	c = 3	c = 1

4. a = 3	5. a = 3	6. a = 1
b = 1	b = 2	b = 3
c = 2	c = 1	c = 2

If your score is 15 to 18, you are easily frustrated. Frustration usually leads to anger and aggression. Letting this anger out is one way to cope with frustrations. Another is to analyze your own reactions. Maybe you are too easily upset by everday trials.

A score of 10 to 14 indicates that you are inclined at times to take it out on others. We all do. The boss bawls us out and we get mad at our subordinates. Usually that only makes it worse. Now we have added another frustration, our own and theirs.

A low score of 6 to 9 is something to be envied. You can take it. Make sure, however, that these reactions are based on experience and wisdom, rather than just on resignation. Sometimes swallowing frustrations can result in outbursts of real anger when you least expect them.

Try to understand why you do things. Focus your energies on a tangible and attainable goal. If you combat frustration with aggression, try to direct that aggressive action into constructive channels.

Let off steam by indulging your anger occasionally. (Some primitive tribes provide for special times when they are allowed to express anger.) If you see that you are deliberately setting out to be cross with people on those days when you are irritated, your anger will begin to look petty and ridiculous to you.

Often we resent people because we cannot fulfill the demands they make on us or because they don't fulfill the expectations we have of them. By becoming aware of these possible problems, we can defuse them before we become frustrated.

What Does Your Body Say About You?

Have you ever noticed the ways you use your arms, your legs, your eyes, your hands, and your head to express yourself?

Your body speaks a special language, but you have to learn to interpret it. We shake hands, for example, to indicate "I don't want to fight." A fist is a sign of anger and aggression, even if you don't hit anybody.

Watch a speaker or politician on TV, and see how he uses his body. It can tell you a lot.

Observe yourself. Do it over a period of a few days or ask someone in your family to do it for you. Some of the questions that follow you may be able to answer right away, others only after such observations.

While this test is only an attempt to help you interpret your most frequent use of various parts of your body and should not be taken too literally, it can indicate how "open" or "closed" you are as a person.

●

1. Your arms, while standing.

    ☐ a. I often fold them over my chest.
    ☒ b. I usually let them hang down.
    ☐ c. I put both, or at least one, on my hips.

2. Your legs, while sitting.

    ☒ a. I cross my knees often.
    ☐ b. I cross my knees and ankles.
    ☐ c. I let my feet rest flat on the floor.

3. Eyes.

    ☒ a. Usually wide open.
    ☐ b. I prefer to keep them half-closed.
    ☐ c. Close them frequently during the day.

4. Head.

    ☒ a. Try to keep it held high.
    ☐ b. Usually slightly tilted to one side or the other.
    ☐ c. Let it hang down.

5. Your hands, especially when you are talking with someone.

    ☒ a. I like to intertwine my fingers often.
    ☐ b. I turn my palms up and have my hands separate.
    ☐ c. I either make a praying gesture or have one hand on top of the other.

6. Total posture.

    ☐ a. I stoop more often than I stand straight.
    ☒ b. I try to keep a reasonably good posture.
    ☐ c. I am rather stiff. I only feel good if my back has a military straightness.

Please turn the page to find out your score and what it means

SCORING

Add your score according to the key below:

1. a = 3	2. a = 2	3. a = 1
b = 1	b = 3	b = 2
c = 2	c = 1	c = 3
4. a = 1	5. a = 3	6. a = 3
b = 2	b = 1	b = 2
c = 3	c = 2	c = 1

If your score is more than 16, you are using most of the parts of your body to express closedness, a self-protective attitude toward others and the world.

A score of 11 to 15 puts you in a category with most of us, a mixture between openness and self-protection. You might be interested in studying which parts of your body are most expressive in one or the other direction.

How Sentimental Are You Compared to Others?

Do you usually cry at weddings? Gush over baby pictures? Long for "the good old days"? Does a story about an orphan saved from hardship by a rich uncle move you to tears?

You may be sentimental. Picture yourself in the following situations. Check the letter of the answer that comes closest to your feelings.

●

1. Listening to an old-time song . . .

   - [ ] a. bores me.
   - [x] b. entertains me.
   - [ ] c. touches me; it brings back memories.

2. At the movies, when a sad scene is portrayed:

   - [ ] a. I generally snicker at the sob stuff.
   - [x] b. If the story's unusually good, I'm moved.
   - [ ] c. I always feel sad, and sometimes I cry.

3. When I receive a letter from an old friend:

   - [ ] a. I read it and then toss it into the wastebasket.
   - [ ] b. Some I keep and finally throw away.
   - [x] c. They're a joy to me. I treasure them for a long time.

4. When people start to talk about the "good old days":

   - [ ] a. I get out of range as soon as possible.
   - [ ] b. If I have something to say, I join the discussion.
   - [x] c. I am likely to agree that those *were* the good old days.

5. Do you keep a family scrapbook?

- ☐ a. No, I can't be bothered.
- ☐ b. Yes, I do, but I seldom look at it.
- ☒ c. Yes, I could spend hours poring over it.

6. I like to celebrate important holidays with my family.

- ☐ a. Sometimes I enjoy being with friends.
- ☐ b. Yes, it's a long-standing family custom.
- ☒ c. I couldn't bear being away from them.

7. When I think about my youth:

- ☐ a. I say, "I'm glad I have grown up."
- ☐ b. I have some regrets, feel some relief.
- ☒ c. I wish I could relive those days.

8. When I read a story with an unhappy ending:

- ☒ a. I think, well, life is sometimes like that.
- ☐ b. I wonder if the ending is true.
- ☐ c. I'm depressed. I prefer happy endings.

Please turn the page to find out your score and what it means

SCORING

For every *a*, give yourself one point; for every *b*, two points, and for every *c*, three points.

A score of around 24: you are extremely sentimental. The average person scores around 16. A score of around 8 suggests you are scornful of sentiment.

Being sentimental is sometimes a substitute for deeply-felt affection or sympathy. The extremely sentimental person may not, as a child, have known real affection. He may be seeking to forget an inner bitterness by distorting and exaggerating what he sees about him. Just as he sentimentalizes the long ago, he weeps for things in the present that he can do nothing about. As he reads in the paper of others' suffering, his deep feelings serve two purposes: first, they make him feel that he is noble in suffering for others; second, they make action unnecessary—for what can one do about a distant stranger's misfortune?

The person who takes enormous pride in *not* being sentimental, like the sentimental individual, has probably also been deprived of genuine love in the past. To him, a display of affection is evidence of weakness. If he could see that real love is possible, he would no longer be afraid to express his own feelings.

Are You Inner- or Outer-Directed?

Some people are influenced primarily by things around them: colors, weather, forms of architecture. Others are influenced mainly by inner motivations: moods, health factors, emotions.

In the following test, check those answers which seem to you to be most appropriate in connection with the various objects. Pick only *one* answer for each.

●

1. Orange VW.

   ☒ a. I could feel good in it.
   ☐ b. A cozy, warm color.
   ☐ c. Trying to be different.

2. English bus (red).

   ☐ a. Very impractical in traffic.
   ☐ b. A symbol of London.
   ☐ c. Excitement, adventure, faraway places.

3. Gray, rainy day.

   ☐ a. I feel depressed, closed in.
   ☐ b. I stay busy, doing "rainy day" things.
   ☐ c. The weather report was wrong again.

4. Sunset.

   ☐ a. A daily phenomenon.
   ☐ b. How quickly the day went by!
   ☐ c. Makes me want to whisper, How beautiful.

5. Beethoven.

  ☐ a. Snow-capped mountain.
  ☐ b. A musical rebel.
  ☐ c. Ecstasy.

6. White horse.

  ☐ a. Corny, widely used picture.
  ☐ b. I would like to ride it.
  ☐ c. A horse lacking pigment.

7. Lake.

  ☐ a. Probably polluted.
  ☐ b. Love to live near one.
  ☐ c. At least fifty feet deep.

8. Zebra.

  ☐ a. A freak of nature.
  ☐ b. Curiously beautiful.
  ☐ c. Blends more easily into landscape for protection.

9. Pink coral.

  ☐ a. Beautiful jewelry.
  ☐ b. Sharp and poisonous.
  ☐ c. Calcified animals.

10. Mozart.

  ☐ a. White birches in the wind.
  ☐ b. Light and airy music.
  ☐ c. Makes your soul dance.

Please turn the page to find out your score and what it means

SCORING

Score yourself according to the following key:

1.		2.		3.		4.		5.	
a = 3		a = 1		a = 3		a = 1		a = 2	
b = 2		b = 2		b = 2		b = 2		b = 1	
c = 1		c = 3		c = 1		c = 3		c = 3	

6.		7.		8.		9.		10.	
a = 2		a = 2		a = 2		a = 3		a = 2	
b = 3		b = 3		b = 3		b = 2		b = 1	
c = 1		c = 1		c = 1		c = 1		c = 3	

If your score is 24 to 30, you have registered the most inner-directed and most romantic reactions. You have projected part of your personality into these pictures. If you looked at an English bus and thought of it only as very impractical in traffic (answer *a*), you show extreme outer-directedness. You are interested only in the *application* of a product, landscape, or situation. By choosing *b,* you show more romanticism, a greater neutrality of reaction; *c* is the most inner-directed answer. Your own emotional reactions were most important.

A score of 17 to 23 represents a mixture of romantic, inner-directed, and sober, outer-directed reactions. You belong to the majority of people, who learn to divide their reactions into practical and sober ones, but still are capable at times of feeling romantic and inner-directed. You can analyze your specific scores in connection with the various objects to see which situations are more inclined to turn you to yourself, whether or not landscapes or colors or animals create more inner- or more outer-directed associations in your mind.

A score of 10 to 16 shows that in most cases you are more inclined to be influenced by facts and cold information. Even when interesting colors or designs are involved, you prefer to pick out the clear-cut description. You are basically an outer-directed person.

Each of these two major qualities of inner- and outer-directedness, or romantic and sober nature, has its application, of course. In general, people with greater inner-directedness tend to be moodier, more creative, and can be happy when alone. They would tend to be in the writing, artistic, or more people-oriented types of occupation.

Outer-directed people also like people, but more as co-workers or persons to be managed. They are more likely to deal in practical matters, are more calculating and better organized.

Both qualities have their role in our modern world. Most of us represent, instead of clear-cut divisions, a mixture of both.

What Do Your Smoking Habits Say About You?

Are you bold or timid, placid or restless, confident or self-conscious? The way you light up, smoke, and hold your cigarette may reveal much about your character.

●

1. How do you light your cigarette?

   ☐ a. Hold your cigarette and strike the match at the same time.
   ☐ b. Go to a man or woman to light your cigarette.
   ☐ c. Wait for a light, and you never wait long.
   ☐ d. Move toward the other person to have him/her light the match, even help light your cigarette.
   ☐ e. Ask the other person to do everything but smoke it for you.

2. How do you hold your cigarette?

   ☐ a. You use your cigarette to punctuate what you say.
   ☐ b. You hold your cigarette quietly, keep it close to you.
   ☐ c. You hold your cigarette with either hand.
   ☐ d. You hide your cigarette in your hand.
   ☐ e. You hold your cigarette delicately.

3. How do you blow the smoke out?

   ☐ a. Let the smoke drift out of your mouth.
   ☐ b. Exhale the smoke as though it were part of you.
   ☐ c. Blow out a lot of smoke at one time.
   ☐ d. Exhale forcefully through your nostrils.
   ☐ e. Let the smoke drift in front of you like a veil.

Please turn the page to find out what your answers mean.

ANALYSIS

1. a. You're not only skillful with your hands, but able to cope with almost any situation. You are a good manager: independent, confident, and competitive. You're particular about whom you include in your circle of friends, and very likely you're the actual or potential leader of the group.
   b. You are probably timid, dependent, or unsure of yourself, but you'll make an effort to have someone else light your cigarette because you're afraid they won't notice you otherwise. You're a good, kindhearted friend—the kind of person people lean on for moral support.
   c. You're vivacious, energetic, and a little bit regal. You come on with class and style. You know what's going on, what's in and what's out. Everyone notices when you enter a room. You expect them to, just as you expect favors and compliments. Usually you get them. As a friend, you're not easy to get along with.
   d. Almost everything else you do is cooperative, too. You respond quickly to a partner's gestures and conversation. A marvelous, lively friend, you are dependable and honest. You don't even know what phony means.
   e. You're easily embarrassed and feel self-conscious around other people. You're never quite sure you are properly dressed. You are a sweet, pleasant friend who likes to be in the background. Always a follower, never a leader, you know how to listen well and are always appreciative.

2. a. You're efficient and energetic, good at organizing projects, committees, groups. When you talk, people pay attention, because you know what you're talking about. You get things done.

b. You're fun-loving, fashionable. If you are a woman, other women probably don't like you very much, although you have a few close women friends. Men are less touchy about each other.

c. Cigarettes are just one of the tools you use to get rid of frustrations. You like to move around, preferably in a car, can't sit still. You don't pay much attention to the people around you.

d. You really think smoking is a dirty habit. But then you think a lot of other things are too. You tend to act as though you should apologize for breathing.

e. You're precise, usually polite. You keep your personal possessions in impeccable order and are always fastidious.

3. a. You're casual, flexible, cooperative, easily persuaded to new ways of looking at a situation, other people's points of view. You give in easily in an argument and are easily flattered by attention.

b. You are most concerned with appearances and how you look to other people. A bit selfish, you hate to let go of things that are yours.

c. This is just one of your attention-getting devices. You're entertaining and people like to be around you. Your clothes are often far-out.

d. One thing is certain: you're not a coward. You are outspoken—gutsy, determined, and tough. Although you're inclined to be a little reserved in dress, speech, and attitudes, you are an open friend who always lets people know where they stand.

e. Although you often say one thing and mean another, you're intriguing because of your imaginative approach to life. Many people think you are mysterious and fascinating.

Are You Living the Kind of Life That Makes You Happy?

For many decades only one major life style—work hard and move up—prevailed for the majority in America. In recent years, however, at least two strong contenders are being tried by many people: a less competitive style that aims chiefly at fulfilling human biological and psychological needs—friendship, family, and community; and a life style based primarily on pleasure principles, without much dependence on outer-directed success goals.

A person may really want the best of all three different styles, a little or a lot more of one than the other, or more of one at one period of life and less at another. The more choice, the more confusing things can become.

The following quiz may help you determine which life style you actually lean to and how well it works for you.

●

1. Imagine that the following goals are reasonably attainable by you. You have a *total* of forty chits' worth of energy to spend achieving all these goals. How many would you spend achieving each goal in the next five years? (Remember, your total cannot exceed 40.)

    Group I
    a. Money. _____
    b. Professional recognition. _____
    c. Possessions. _____

    Group II
    a. Love. _____
    b. Friendship, community involvement. _____
    c. Family involvement. _____

    Group III
    a. Pleasure. _____
    b. Travel. _____
    c. New experiences. _____

2. Each of the phrases below describes a basic life tempo. If you could play your life's tune out for the next ten years, which tempo would you pace it to?

☐ a. Slow waltz.
☐ b. Gradual acceleration.
☐ c. Erratic, dynamic.
☐ d. Quiet, pastoral.

3. What are your plans for the future? Check off how far ahead you are making plans in these areas:

	1 YEAR OR LESS	2 YEARS	3 YEARS	4 YEARS	5 YEARS OR MORE
a. Money	____	____	____	____	____
b. Advancement	____	____	____	____	____
c. Travel	____	____	____	____	____
d. Friends *	____	____	____	____	____
e. Leisure and hobbies	____	____	____	____	____
f. Education	____	____	____	____	____

* In terms of being, staying, or moving into a community close to friends, joining clubs, etc.

4. To what extent would you be emotionally involved in each of these situations?

a. A large, fun party.
☐ (1) Very much involved.
☐ (2) Indifferent.
☐ (3) Cold.

b. A peaceful, rustic village.
☐ (1) Very much involved.
☐ (2) Indifferent.
☐ (3) Cold.

c. Bullfight.
- [ ] (1) Very much involved.
- [ ] (2) Indifferent.
- [ ] (3) Cold.

d. Airplane trip.
- [ ] (1) Very much involved.
- [ ] (2) Indifferent.
- [ ] (3) Cold.

e. Desk in a library.
- [ ] (1) Very much involved.
- [ ] (2) Indifferent.
- [ ] (3) Cold.

5. On the calendar below indicate your prevailing mood, as nearly as you can recall, for each day of last week. (If a crisis like a serious illness or an unusual personal problem occurred, skip last week and choose a more average one.) Use a + for a good optimistic mood, a ~ sign for indifference and a − for a negative and pessimistic feeling. Then add up the number of days when you felt positive and optimistic, indifferent, or pessimistic.

	Sun.	Mon.	Tues.	Wed.	Thur.	Fri.	Sat.
Average Week							

Please turn the page to find out your score and what it means

SCORING

The first four parts of the quiz indicate which life style or styles you have chosen. The fifth throws some light on how that life style is working for you.

1. This is the basic determining test. Group I consists of cultural and outer-directed goals—professional recognition, possessions, money. If you have more chits in Group I than in any other, you have chosen a possession- and achievement-directed life style.

If you have more in Group II, you belong in a self-oriented, peaceful life style, in which love, friendship, community commitment, and family life provide fulfillment of your own human needs.

If you have a majority of chits in Group III, your life style is based on the pleasure principle; you mean to get as much out of this life as possible. You are interested largely in the inner experiences, independent of outside, goal-oriented forces.

If you are more or less equally balanced among the three groups, don't be confused. The better the balance, the more flexible and open your life style is. You see the best in all of them.

2, 3, and 4. The next three parts help to prove further your attachment to the life style 1 indicated for you. Check yourself out according to the group you fit into. If you are well balanced between groups in 1, you may find that on the secondary level explored in 2, 3, and 4, your preferences are more weighted to one life style than to another.

Possession- and Achievement-Directed Life Style:
2: b
3: a, b, and f
4: a. (1)
    c. (1)
    d. (1)

Self-Oriented, Peaceful Life Style:
2: d
3: d and e
4: b. (1)
    e. (1)

Pleasure-Principle Life Style:
2: a and/or c
3: e and f, possibly c
4: a. (1)
   b. (1)

5. This part reveals something about your general attitude toward life, which in turn affects how you live it.

For example, the achievement-oriented person who scores extremely pessimistically—say, six days out of seven—may be afraid or questioning his or her goals, either because the person has seen that material success does not automatically assure happiness, or maybe because he or she feels inadequate to these goals. A preponderance of positive days might mean that this person has made a dynamic, achievement-oriented choice that is thoroughly enjoyable and rewarding.

Someone who has chosen a self-oriented peaceful style but who has more indifferent than positive or negative days is probably more passive than peaceful, and tends to let life dominate him or her instead of the other way around. On the other hand, if that person had marked more positive days than indifferent ones, his or her peacefulness would be of a dynamic nature, a positive working for peace rather than a giving in to anything that would provide it.

Another example: A person who leans toward the pleasure-principle style, but marks more days pessimistically, would probably be more of a "cop-out" artist than a real pleasure seeker. In the extreme, he or she would be a person who appeared to love pleasure simply because anything else would involve too much work. A positive score of days combined with the pleasure-principle style could be interpreted as a real desire to enjoy life, knowing that it might well be at the expense of achievement and money.

It would be impossible here to cover all the possible combinations. But the above examples should provide you with some technique for analyzing your own variations correctly. The main purpose of part 5 is to direct you to some life accounting, a kind of inventory taking of how well your life style may be working for you. If your attitude is overwhelmingly pessimistic or indifferent, you should try to reevaluate your chosen life style and your attitude to see where the discrepancies are.

How Gullible Are You?

Most of us are convinced that we can easily resist a sales pitch, that we can spot a phony approach a mile away. Good salesmen know that the person who thinks he offers the most resistance and who declares he is not a sucker is often the one most easily sold.

The test that follows will help you to decide whether you really are gullible or not. Check the answer you select.

●

1. You are planning to buy a chair, and you see three chairs advertised. One is called "Classic Style," priced at $38.50; the second one, "Form Fit," at $42.90; and the third, "Back Health," at $55.00. You are told they are only slightly different from each other. Which one would you buy, without seeing pictures of them?

    ☐ a. Classic Style $38.50
    ☐ b. Form Fit $42.90
    ☐ c. Back Health $55.00

2. Three men are candidates for political office. After reading the descriptions for each, which one would you work for?

    ☐ a. *Mr. Ludwig:* Very well-liked in his district, young and progressive, has interesting hobbies like collecting old tools, is happily married, outgoing, and interested in helping others.
    ☐ b. *Mr. Jolly:* Over forty, divorced, friendly, very systematic, has a good voting record, is somewhat of a swinger.
    ☐ c. *Mr. Seaforth:* Spends a lot of time studying all aspects of various issues, antagonizes people occasionally, but sticks to his guns once he is convinced of the merits of a problem.

3. You have to choose among the following suits or dresses. Which one would you pick?

☐ a. Designed by Pierre Cardin or Christian Dior.
☐ b. Includes essential elements of the latest fashion.
☐ c. An original copy of name designer.
☐ d. Indistinguishable from a famous name designer.
☐ e. Good-looking, elegant.

4. The following are financial statements of several different companies. In which would you like to invest?

☐ a. "Our volume of sales has continued increasing at a rate of 10 percent every year. In 1968, it was $1,965,510; in 1969, $2,001,230; and in 1970, $2,109,620. We hope to continue at the same rate."
☐ b. "Our profit picture has been very satisfactory. It was 9 percent of our total volume in 1968, 10 percent in 1969, and 8 percent in 1970."
☐ c. "We have been consistently selling 5 percent more units every year."
☐ d. "We have maintained our profit margin by averaging out over the last five years, and have also increased our volume in line with the population growth in our line of products."

5. Pretend that you have just arrived at a party, and there is a man standing alone to one side. Everybody seems to be shunning him and whispering about him. What would you do?

☐ a. Go over to him and find out more about him.
☐ b. Inquire from the rest of the group what is the matter with him and then decide.
☐ c. Decide not to get involved and concentrate on others in the group for conversation.
☐ d. Make a special effort to be nice to him, to spite the others.

6. Someone tells you about an absolutely marvelous vacation spot. They had a wonderful time. The food was good, the price right. What would you do?

☐ a. I would ask for more details—what they did all day and the kind of people they met. This way I could decide whether their vacation ideal corresponds with mine.

☐ b. It is difficult to find a good place. I would go there without much hesitation.

☐ c. I would consider one or two additional alternatives before committing myself.

☐ d. I hardly ever believe other people's stories about vacation spots. I have had too many bad experiences.

7. Imagine that you are taking a drive in an unfamiliar area. You inquire about the best road for getting to a particular location. You are told by a local person about a rather dangerous but picturesque and short road. He tells you not to take it, but to take another road that is much longer, but not so dangerous. What would your reaction be?

☐ a. To ask someone else about the shorter road.
☐ b. To accept this person's advice and take the safer road.
☐ c. To take the supposedly dangerous road, relying on your own judgment.

8. If your marital partner were in a good mood because he or she had had a good day, but you were in a bad mood, what would most likely happen?

☐ a. My bad mood would affect my partner, and he or she would be in a bad mood too.

☐ b. My partner's good mood would affect me, and my mood would change.

☐ c. I would stay in my bad mood, regardless of my partner's mood.

☐ d. I would get into a worse mood because of his or her good mood.

9. If you were to see the following headlines in your newspaper, which article would you honestly read first?

☐ a. Peace in the Middle East
☐ b. POLICEMAN KILLED IN RIOT
☐ c. DOLLAR VALUE FLUCTUATES

10. An acquaintance tells you he has invited several famous people to his apartment. He asks you to come too. What would you do?

☐ a. I would ask him who the famous people were.
☐ b. I would simply go.
☐ c. I would go, but warn him that if no one famous was there I would leave.
☐ d. I would call a couple of the people he mentioned to check whether he was telling me the truth.

11. Read the following statement:

The foremost development in the field of forestry came from the science of biology.

How many *f*'s are there?

☐ a. 3
☐ b. 4
☐ c. 5

Please turn the page to find out your score and what it means

SCORING

Add your score according to the following key:

1. a = 1	2. a = 3	3. a = 3	4. a = 3
b = 2	b = 2	b = 2	b = 2
c = 3	c = 1	c = 4	c = 2
		d = 3	d = 1
		e = 1	
5. a = 1	6. a = 2	7. a = 2	8. a = 1
b = 2	b = 3	b = 3	b = 2
c = 3	c = 2	c = 1	c = 1
d = 2	d = 1		d = 3
9. a = 1	10. a = 1	11. a = 3	
b = 2	b = 3	b = 2	
c = 3	c = 2	c = 1	
	d = 2		

If you scored between 10 and 15, you are not very gullible. If you had checked the facts, you would have seen that in question 1, for example, you were being sold more or less the same chair. In 2, Mr. Seaforth (c) was the only candidate whose qualifications as a public candidate were discussed. In 3, the answer which showed the most gullibility was c because, if you read it carefully, you would have seen that it was only double talk. In question 4 a, there really was no increase of 10 percent in sales volume. In 9, if you answered c, you were influenced by the size of the headline.

If you scored 15 to 25, you are about as gullible as most of us are.

If your score is between 25 and 33, you had better think of ways of curing yourself of your gullibility. Often the gullible person really likes to be taken in because he then can blame somebody else for his mistakes. You might make note of some of these suggestions:

1. Always check facts first; don't believe the easy promise.

2. Be ready to make your own mistakes, and don't just listen to somebody else's advice.

3. Find out the real reasons for your gullibility. Are you just too lazy to think things through, or do you prefer to blame others?

How Much Do Your Moods Control You and How Much Do You Control Your Moods?

We all have moods. They can ruin our day, our work, and often our relations with others. Moods, if they govern your life too much, can be costly as far as they affect your work. Being in a bad mood robs you of initiative and makes you difficult to get along with.

Some among us react very quickly to given situations. A gray sky can produce a gray mood. Others retain their even tempers regardless of what happens. Often we don't even know why we are in a good mood or in a bad one. Most of us, however, have used being in a good mood or a bad mood as an excuse to do something or act in some way that would otherwise not seem acceptable.

It might be interesting for you to find out what your most likely reactions are when faced with various "moody" situations.

●

1. For some time you have been kept waiting for a special assignment or a promotion. How do you usually react to such a postponement?

☐ a. It makes me restless and irritable.
☐ b. I am patient. I can wait. My mood is fairly steady.
☐ c. I would not be cheerful. I might take some action in another field, to fight my disappointment.

2. You criticize someone's work. You yourself are surprised at how violent your reaction is. Later on you analyze what happened. Which one of these explanations would apply most frequently?

☐ a. I was in a bad mood and must have taken it out on the poor person whose work I tore apart.
☐ b. I was fair in my appraisal; I had reasons to be critical.
☐ c. I should have waited and looked at the person's work a second time, before passing judgment.

3. Which one of these descriptions would your friends or your spouse be most likely to apply to *you?*

☐ a. He/She has frequent ups and downs, and can influence a whole group of people with his/her own feelings.

☐ b. You would never know what mood he/she is in. It does not affect his/her work or behavior.

☐ c. She/He would talk about the bad or good mood she/he is in, but almost as if it were someone else to whom it was happening.

4. Which one of these abstract figures would best describe the kind of mood you are in most of the time?

☐ a. An upward-swinging, happy curve.
☐ b. A wave pattern, with many ups and downs.
☐ c. Heavy, droopy, downward line.

5. On top of several other things that have gone wrong today, a waiter is rude to you. How does it usually affect you?

☐ a. I shrug it off. These people probably have to put up with a lot.

☐ b. It can really make me explode. For a few hours afterward I am almost depressed about how nasty people can be.

☐ c. I will try to do something nice to cheer myself up, like buying something or reminding myself of nice people.

6. You hear or read about the senseless murder of a decent person. How do you react?

☐ a. It is part of life. I am shocked, but forget about it soon. I cannot get upset about everything.

☐ b. It can ruin my whole day.
☐ c. I have immunized myself against such events.

Please turn the page to find out your score and what it means

SCORING

Add your scores according to the following key:

1. a = 3	2. a = 3	3. a = 3
b = 1	b = 1	b = 1
c = 2	c = 2	c = 2
4. a = 3	5. a = 1	6. a = 2
b = 1	b = 3	b = 3
c = 3	c = 2	c = 1

Your highest possible score, 16 to 18, shows you are a person very much controlled by your own moods. A score of 10 to 15 indicates you are a person who has changing moods but is not so vulnerable that everything and everybody around him is influenced. A score of 6 to 9 shows you are a very controlled person who has moods but does not permit them to interfere with the rest of his life.

Are You Prejudiced?

Another black mayor! Another Italian a Mafia kingpin! Newsmen covering election results distort facts! Another race riot!

Many people are angry, frightened, frustrated. Many are also prejudiced. In general, it is no longer considered chic to show prejudice—but it is still there. Often it comes out in subtle ways. How often have you heard—or made—comments like "Of course, a Puerto Rican," "a woman driver," "typical for a man," or "no wonder—an aggressive Jew"?

Prejudice is undesirable not only because it is immoral or unfair, but also for a much more practical reason. Decisions we make based on prejudice are more harmful to *us* than to the person or group against whom the prejudice is directed. If you, yourself, belong to a group that arouses prejudice, you have a personal stake in doing something about eradicating it.

The following quiz may help you locate your own real—but often subtle—prejudices. Try to be as honest as you can.

•

1. Which word in the left-hand column do you immediately associate with a word in the right-hand column (for instance, "low" with "reporter")? If you feel that a word in the left-hand column doesn't necessarily apply to a specific word in the right-hand column—or might apply to a number of words in the right-hand column—do not connect it.

slim	liberal
genuine	conservative
hollow	boss
fat	Mexican
dark	Negro
good	reporter
strong	Presbyterian
top	Englishman
poor	salesman
crazy	Catholic
lazy	American
low	Chinese
light	Irishman
tall	fireman
sneaky	accountant
honest	mechanic
reserved	politician
corrupt	builder

2. These are the Presidents of the U.S. up to 1980. What is your *immediate* reaction?

   KENNEDY   JOHNSON   NIXON   FORD   BLACK MAN

   ☐ a. I would leave the country if it happened.
   ☐ b. I hope it never happens; but if it does, I will have to accept it.
   ☐ c. If he is a good man, why not?

3. You are in a hotel. It is late—1 A.M. You want to get some sleep. You hear a party or loud noise going on next door. What is your first thought?

☐ a. They must be young.
☐ b. They are probably blacks or Puerto Ricans.
☐ c. They must be drunk or stoned.

4. Somebody is arranging a blind date for you. When you meet the young woman/man, she/he turns out to be black (or white, if you are black). What is your reaction?

☐ a. You are pleasantly surprised because of the new experience.
☐ b. You try to make the best of it.
☐ c. You use an excuse and try to get out of the date.

5. At a party you see a woman with a see-through blouse and nothing under it. What is your reaction?

☐ a. This is outrageous.
☐ b. I would never do it, but it is quite intriguing.
☐ c. Maybe I will try it, too, one of these days (or date a girl dressed that way).

6. "Most people are happiest if they can get away with as little work as possible." What is your first reaction?

☐ a. Agree.
☐ b. Disagree.
☐ c. Partially right.

Now assume this statement was written by an employer, an employee, or an authority on work. Would your reactions be the same? Check your reactions for each person.

(1) Employer
☐ a. I still agree.
☐ b. I still disagree.
☐ c. I still think it's partially right.

(2) Employee
- ☐ a. I still agree.
- ☐ b. I still disagree.
- ☐ c. I still think it's partially right.

(3) Authority on work
- ☐ a. I still agree.
- ☐ b. I still disagree.
- ☐ c. I still think it's partially right.

7. You are dining in an elegant restaurant. At another table you see a very casually dressed family. What is your reaction?

- ☐ a. They must be very small-town; obviously they don't know how to behave or dress appropriately.
- ☐ b. They must be very rich and don't have to care.
- ☐ c. They wanted to be comfortable and did what pleased them most.

Please turn the page to find out your score and what it means

SCORING

1. If you quickly associated between one and 10 of the words in the left column with words in the right column, then your score to be used for the final scoreboard is 5. Should you have made between 10 and 18 such stereotyped connections, give yourself a score of 7. If you did not connect a concept or if you felt that it could just as easily be connected with various words, then you are probably not prejudiced. Give yourself a score of 2.

2. a = 3	3. a = 2	4. a = 1	5. a = 3
b = 2	b = 3	b = 2	b = 2
c = 1	c = 1	c = 3	c = 1

6. If your reaction stayed the same, no matter who said it, your score is 0. If you changed your mind depending on who said it, give yourself one point for *each* time your reaction changed.

7. a = 3
   b = 2
   c = 1

Now add up your total score for all items.
If your total score is between 23 and 25, you should be

aware of the fact that while you intellectually accept the need for objectivity, many of your daily actions and decisions are colored by prejudices and stereotypes. Before jumping to conclusions, it would be a good idea to ask yourself, "Did I say or do this just because I have preconceived notions, or because my facts were correct?"

A score of 16 to 22 is average. Few people are so "clean" in their convictions that they don't ever let their reactions be colored by stereotypes: "Just like a man," or "Only a black man (or white man) would do this." Even our newspaper or TV reports quite often include subconscious bias indicated by the use of certain words and selective photographs. Number 6 measures the degree to which a statement becomes more or less true or important to you, depending on who or what kind of person says it. The more often this kind of change occurs, the more susceptible you are to prejudice.

If you score 10 to 15, you must count yourself in the rare group (if you don't lie to yourself) who have trained themselves to look first at the objective facts before judging. You also have a duty to educate other people against using prejudice to come to easy conclusions about issues and people.

Many tragedies—national as well as personal—can be avoided if we all trained ourselves to be free from the cobwebs and chains of bias.

Do You Really Know How to Relax?

Relax! Or have you forgotten how to? Relaxation, after all, is probably at least as much a state of mind as a physical state.

Some people are racing even when they go on vacation. They "eat up" the miles in their cars. They "do" Europe in five days and are proud of it. Even keeping a garden becomes an exercise in a Dale Carnegie course: unless your tomatoes are bigger than your neighbors', you aren't satisfied. What starts out as a relaxation becomes a challenge.

How do *you* rate as a "relaxing" artist? Study the eight situations described below. Then, for each, check the item that best describes your own reaction.

•

1. Man playing golf.

   ☐ a. He's trying a long, over-the-water shot to cut his score.
   ☑ b. He's "in the swing," enjoying the shot he's making.
   ☐ c. He's pressing for a long shot.

2. A couple shopping in the Bahamas.

   ☐ a. They're enjoying the exotic scenes and customs.
   ☐ b. They're curious about merchandise made by the natives.
   ☐ c. They think they get better value at home.

3. A man sitting in an easy chair, reading.

   ☐ a. He's catching up on necessary reading—the comfortable way.
   ☐ b. He doesn't care what he reads. He just relaxes.
   ☐ c. He is determined to get through his book before vacation ends.

4. A woman bending over in her garden.

   ☐ a. She would like to rest, but is conscientious and finishes weeding.

   ☐ b. She stops because she wants to.

   ☐ c. She's annoyed because she hasn't finished, but stops because she's tired.

5. Family in a car, driving down a highway.

   ☐ a. They just stop and eat, or go on and drive, as they please.

   ☐ b. They have to take a "time out."

   ☐ c. They want to keep to their schedule and eat the quickest way.

6. A man in a darkroom, bending over trays of developing fluid.

   ☐ a. Photography is his new hobby; he'll spend hours enjoying it.

   ☐ b. He has to finish enlargements, which he postponed so often.

   ☐ c. He likes what he's doing, but is somewhat tired.

7. A couple locking up a cabin and getting into their car.

   ☐ a. They hate to leave and feel their vacation was really much too short.

   ☐ b. They're figuring the cost of the trip.

   ☐ c. They are making some new plans for when they get back home.

8. Two friends having drinks on a terrace by the ocean.

   ☐ a. They are enjoying the moment, the place, and each other.

   ☐ b. They discuss their future and what will become of them.

   ☐ c. They feel they wasted the afternoon and should have done something valuable.

Please turn the page to find out your score and what it means

SCORING

Add your score according to the following key:

1. a = 2	2. a = 3	3. a = 2	4. a = 1
b = 3	b = 2	b = 3	b = 3
c = 1	c = 1	c = 1	c = 2
5. a = 3	6. a = 3	7. a = 2	8. a = 3
b = 2	b = 1	b = 1	b = 2
c = 1	c = 2	c = 3	c = 1

If your score is 8 to 10, you had better let up. Your life is too hectic. You don't trust yourself enough to relax. A score of 11 to 14 is better, but is still a sign of tense efforts, which in the end slow you down rather than help you. A score of 15 to 20 brings you over to the category of those people who can see the lighter side of life—who don't see a challenge in each game of golf. You really know how to relax if your score is 21 to 24. You are a good vacationer. You know how to let go.

The best way to enjoy your vacation is to use it as a training period in relaxation, if you have not already learned how to let go. If you were well advanced in the art of relaxation even before your vacation, you can consider your vacation a refresher course.

Find out when you are really happy. It is then that you are closest to your real self. Relaxation means that you are being yourself. Relaxation, in its broadest sense, consists of living life for its own sake, whether working or vacationing—to enjoy every minute of it as an interesting, creative experience.

What Does Your Telephone Manner Tell About You?

Your telephone manner, like your body language and your handwriting, tells a great deal about the kind of person you are and how you relate to others. Often, we are even more expressive of ourselves on the phone, because we can't see the other person.

Just as not all of us write exactly the same way, not all of us hold the telephone exactly the same way. Through these little differences our individuality shows itself.

What can you tell when you watch somebody using the phone? What can you learn about yourself from the way you handle it? A telephone conversation is a form of interpersonal relationship: you are communicating with somebody else. While a lot depends, of course, on what is being discussed, the quiz that follows includes some of the most typical kinds of telephone behavior. Check the three positions that apply to you most frequently:

●

☐   1. Person holding phone in a stiff and formal manner.
☐   2. Speaker leaning toward invisible partner at other end of the line.
☒   3. While phoning, legs hanging over the arm of a chair, or sitting on floor.
☒   4. Vivid movements of arms and facial expressions.
☐   5. Leans into telephone mouthpiece, but earpiece not too closely held.
☐   6. Almost immersed in the mouthpiece.
☐   7. Listening piece removed from ear.
☐   8. Speaking and listening pieces equal distance from ear.
☒   9. Ear close to listening piece.
☐ 10. Huddled around phone.
☐ 11. Sitting on edge of desk.
☐ 12. Hand over mouthpiece while listening.

Please turn the page to find out your score and what it means

SCORING

If you checked 1, 3, 6, 7, or 8, you are a "correct" speaker. You try to keep your distance. You are interested primarily in being heard and impressing others. You like to play a teacher's role, and are not too concerned with the opinions and reactions of the other person.

If you checked 4, 5, 9, 11, or 12, you always try to establish contact. You are aware of the other person's presence; you are probably a good salesman. Distances do not bother you.

If you checked 2, 5, 10, or 11, you have a balanced attitude. You are conscious of your own position and ideas. You are listening and thinking, considering your own and your telephone partner's opinions carefully. You talk as if your partner were present. You have a good ability to establish contact.

Of course these telephone gestures should be interpreted together with other aspects of body language. But telephone behavior is a good indicator of deeper attitudes, because of the extra effort necessary to bridge a gap.

PART TWO

How Well Do You Get Along with Others?

In the first section we asked you to take an inventory of yourself.

In this section you will have a chance to get a better picture of your relationships with others. Few of us live by ourselves. Many of our characteristics reveal themselves through contact with other people.

How Well-Liked Do You Think You Are?

Most of us would like to think we are well-liked. Then, every so often, we hear something said about us that surprises or shocks us, and we wonder just how well-liked we really are.

Imagine you could find out what people really think about you by looking into a psychological mirror.

The following quiz may be just such a mirror. First, take it yourself, indicating what you think your popularity is. Then hand the quiz to one or more people who know you well enough to express an opinion about you.

The scoring detailed at the end of the quiz should be interesting from two points of view: how you evaluate your popularity, and how your friends evaluate it.

●

1. A group is trying to get a party together. They have five choices. Which choice do you think you would be?

   - ☐ a. 1st choice
   - ☐ b. 2nd choice
   - ☒ c. 3rd choice
   - ☐ d. 4th choice
   - ☐ e. 5th choice

2. You find some files containing the following secret evaluations of various people. Which one would apply to you?

   - ☐ a. Very aggressive, wants to get ahead at all costs, rather a loner.
   - ☒ b. Seems to know everybody and gets along well with peers and with groups above and below. Tries too hard to be liked by everybody.
   - ☐ c. Moody, can be charming, but often turns on others quite unexpectedly; does things satisfactorily, but rather routinely.

3. You get yourself in trouble (shoplifting in a store or smoking pot, for example) and you are caught. How would your friends react?

    ☐ a. They would abandon me.
    ☒ b. A few would go out of their way to help me.
    ☐ c. Most of them would be superficially friendly; they would generally stay away.

4. First list as many good and bad qualities (kind, loving, resentful, loud, etc.) about yourself as you can think of (create more spaces, if you need them). Then ask ten of your friends or acquaintances to make lists of the best and worst qualities about you. Do not show your friends your own checklist. It is important to know which qualities they pick spontaneously.

Good qualities	Bad qualities
1 _____	1 _____
2 _____	2 _____
3 _____	3 _____
4 _____	4 _____
5 _____	5 _____
6 _____	6 _____
7 _____	7 _____
8 _____	8 _____
9 _____	9 _____
10 _____	10 _____

5. You make a very awkward, very loud remark during a party, a real faux pas, such as, "Your *third* marriage broke up?" How would most of the other people at the party react if they heard you?

    ☒ a. That's typical; he/she always talks too much.
    ☐ b. Could have been more subtle, but he/she is right.
    ☐ c. Certainly not a hypocrite.

6. Which of your qualities do you think you should work on to improve? List them. Count them up. How many did you list?

    ☐ a. Four to five.
    ☐ b. None.
    ☐ c. Almost everything.

7. On a scale—say, a thermometer—how would you rate yourself as far as emotional warmth or coolness, including passion, is concerned? Jot the "temperature" down, and then ask your friends what they think.

8. You meet someone for the first time. You are not sure what impression you made. Then you meet him/her four more times. Do you feel that he/she is more likely to:

   ☐ a. Improve his impression of you?
   ☐ b. Have the same impression?
   ☐ c. Lower his appreciation?

9. You are told that somebody said something nasty about you. Are you more likely to:

   ☐ a. Accept the judgment and be depressed?
   ☐ b. Look for something bad in the other person?
   ☐ c. Agree with some of the criticism but try to explain to yourself or others why you are that way or even make fun of yourself?

Please turn the page to find out your score and what it means

SCORING

How well-liked you think you are is often a sign of your own security or insecurity. Usually if you like yourself, the chances are others will like you too. No one is perfect, and we often like a person better if he or she makes occasional mistakes.

Let us discuss the individual questions.

1. If you feel that you will always be first choice in being selected for a party, this is almost as much a sign of feeling inferior as if you are always the last choice. Superiority and inferiority feelings are closely related. Your best score is probably somewhere between third and fourth choice.

2. Choice *b* is the best from the viewpoint of being well-liked, although it may not necessarily help your career. Items *a* and *c* show insecurity and doubts.

3. If you chose *b,* you are very lucky in your choice of friends, but be sure you are not kidding yourself. A casual but worthwhile test might be to try out a similar story on your friends, pretending that it really happened. If, on the other hand, you feel that *a* applies to your friends, you obviously don't think much of your friends and, indirectly, of yourself.

4. First, check carefully how many positive against negative qualities you can think of. If you have thought of a few more positive than negative qualities, you are a well-balanced person. If one or the other column outweighs the other by more than 50 percent, you may have problems with either superiority or inferiority feelings.

Even more important is to analyze what kinds of qualities you have chosen. For example, you could have among most of your positive qualities intellectual aspects such as bright, good memory, etc., and among your negative qualities more emotional ones such as impatient, irascible, etc.

5. a. You are unsure of yourself.
   b. A fairly good opinion.
   c. May be wishful thinking.

6. a. *Within reason,* the more qualities—say, four to five—you think you should improve on, the better balanced you are, the better you like yourself.
   b. If you checked "None" it should worry you. Nobody is *that* perfect.
   c. Again, you are going too far in the other direction.

7. This rating has less to do with frigidity or pure passion than with the normal designation of an individual as a warm, outgoing or an aloof person. A good rating would be between +50 and +70.

8. We usually prefer a *gradual* improvement in the impression we make on others, rather than immediate compliments. Thus:
   a would give you a good score.
   c would indicate that you are hiding your real self or putting on a good show.
   b is not bad but less exciting.

9. The best rating would be *c; a* and *b* are signs of insecurity.

Even more important than your own evaluations is the discovery of how many discrepancies there are between your self-judgments and the judgments of your friends, and how much you're bothered by these differences. How defensive, annoyed, and insulted do you feel about these differences? Or do you feel, simply: How interesting. I better do something about the impression I seem to create, whether it corresponds to my own evaluation or not?

How Sexy Are You?

What do we really mean when we say about someone that he or she is "sexy"?

For some people, sexiness has to do mainly with another person's physical appearance. For some, it's another person's state of dress—or undress. Others believe sexiness is in a person's eyes or body language. And still others will tell you sexiness is a state of mind, and the ability to communicate that state of mind to someone else.

Probably, for any two people, sexiness is a combination of many of these things, some of which will be more, some less, important, given the circumstances, the people, the setting, the kind of relationship, and many other variables.

The purpose of the quiz that follows is to help you discover what *you* think sexiness is and how sexy you think you are. Sexual standards and customs are, of course, changing all the time, and most are relative anyway. But we hope we've covered enough bases and asked enough of the right questions to give you some insight into yourself.

To make the test meaningful, you should first take it yourself, then have your partner take it. The degree of discrepancy or agreement between the two scores will add an interesting and significant dimension to this analysis.

If you are not sure about the answers, don't try to make them up, guess, or lie. Observe yourself over the next two or three weeks and then take the test.

●

1. After the sex act do you feel:

☐ a. Depressed?
☐ b. Happy and tender?
☐ c. Indifferent?

2. What do you usually say after a satisfactory sex experience?

   ☐ a. Compliment your partner.
   ☐ b. Comment on both your prowess.
   ☐ c. Pat *yourself* on the back through a remark or behavior.

3. Do you consider yourself sexually "creative," that is, do you make a special effort to try new positions or techniques?

   ☐ a. Almost never.
   ☐ b. Occasionally.
   ☐ c. As often as possible.

4. Of the *total time* of a sexual experience, which statement comes closest to describing how much time is devoted to pre-sex play, the actual sex act, and the after-sex period?

   ☐ a. Pre-sex play is generally long.
   ☐ b. After-sex period is generally short.
   ☐ c. After-sex period or the pre-sex play is generally short.

5. Have you made sexual overtures toward a man or a woman:

   ☐ a. Directly?
   ☐ b. Indirectly?
   ☐ c. Never?

6. Do you think you are pretty much the same kind of person, with the same kind of personality, during the sex act as you are otherwise?

   ☐ a. The same.
   ☐ b. Somewhat different.
   ☐ c. Completely different.

7. Check the *one* statement that best describes your attitude in most instances.

   ☐ a. I make sure *I* have fun in sex.
   ☐ b. My partner should have pleasure, even if I don't.
   ☐ c. Both of us usually try to achieve fulfillment.

8. If your partner has difficulties, do you blame:

☐ a. Yourself?
☐ b. Him or her?
☐ c. Both of you?

9 How do you feel about talking about sex?

☐ a. Don't like to; it's embarrassing.
☐ b. It's not easy, but it's important.
☐ c. I love to talk about it; it's a real turn-on.

10. Which parts of your body do you consider erotic? List them in the space below.

_____   _____
_____   _____
_____   _____

11. I am more aroused during sex if I can imagine or think about:

☐ a. My real partner.
☐ b. A famous actor or highly desirable man or woman.
☐ c. My partner, but changed (richer, more tender, younger, etc.).

12. I respond better if my partner is:

☐ a. Aggressive.
☐ b. Needing protection.
☐ c. Tender, but responsive.

Please turn the page to find out your score and what it means

SCORING

1. a = 2 b = 3 c = 1	2. a = 2 b = 3 c = 1	3. a = 1 b = 2 c = 3	4. a = 3 b = 2 c = 1
5. a = 2 b = 3 c = 1	6. a = 3 b = 2 c = 1	7. a = 2 b = 1 c = 3	8. a = 2 b = 1 c = 3
9. a = 1 b = 2 c = 3	10. 1 point if only one part named; 2 points if 2 parts named; 4 points if 3 or more parts named	11. a = 3 b = 1 c = 2	12. a = 2 b = 1 c = 3

If you scored 28 or more, you are probably well-balanced, consider sex a partnership affair, and have a high degree of creativity.

A 20-27 score: you could probably profit from a more relaxed attitude toward sex. A lot depends, of course, on how this score is composed. If you checked a in 1, 2, 3; b in 4, a in 5, c in 6; a in 7; a or b in 8; a in 9; b in 11; and a in 12—you could be either too submissive or too domineering in sex.

If your score is below 20, your sex life is either inhibited or you display an indifferent attitude. There is, of course, no absolute norm—but if you look back over your individual answers, you may find the specific areas that could use some improvement.

How Much Trust Do You Have in Others?

Some people, particularly after they have been disappointed by others, decide it is better and safer not to trust anybody. They believe that to think the worst, to assume that selfishness is a basic human motivation, is usually safer. Whenever someone tries to be nice to them, they wonder what is really behind it.

How much trust do *you* have in others and in yourself? Check the appropriate answer:

●

1. You read this headline in a newspaper: "Important Figure Swears He Never Took a Bribe." What is your reaction?

   ☐ a. He is clever and has learned to conceal and cover up his activities. We'll never learn the truth.
   ☐ b. He has been unjustly accused. It has happened before.
   ☐ c. I can see the next headline: "Mr. X Indicted."

2. React to this headline: "Leftist Lawyer Vindicated. Previous Conviction of Perjury Found Unjust."

   ☐ a. I always thought he was innocent.
   ☐ b. I still don't trust him.
   ☐ c. He just had better lawyers now to defend him.

3. "Elderly Bondholders Lose Millions in Financial Scandal."

   ☐ a. The investors should have investigated the company selling the bonds more carefully. Too many people are gullible.
   ☐ b. Everything may have been all right in the beginning. Things just went sour.
   ☐ c. It was too good. Any return like that usually involves crooked business.

4. A young couple hired a contractor to build a house for them. Completion date was six months. Despite all promises it is still unfinished. What would your comment to them be?

☐ a. They should never have trusted the contractor. They are always late or cheat.

☐ b. It is probably not the contractor's fault. He has his own problems.

☐ c. So what? A few weeks longer will be forgotten by them a couple of years from now.

5. Police deny having killed a young demonstrator. Shots were fired from the crowd. What is the true story?

☐ a. Police always protect each other. Why should they get themselves into trouble?

☐ b. Such accidents do happen. Rioters often kill their own. I would believe the policemen's story.

☐ c. Police may just have overreacted. Their warning shots went astray.

6. Management tells its workers their profits are too low to grant a pay raise.

☐ a. I would believe them. It is in their own interest to keep their workers happy.

☐ b. That's what they always say. The more they can keep for themselves, the better they like it.

☐ c. They should open their books and ask the workers to help improve the situation, if their story of low profits is true.

Please turn the page to find out your score and what it means

SCORING

Add your scores according to the following key:

1. a = 2	2. a = 1	3. a = 2
b = 1	b = 2	b = 1
c = 3	c = 3	c = 3
4. a = 3	5. a = 3	6. a = 1
b = 1	b = 1	b = 3
c = 2	c = 2	c = 2

A score of 15 to 18 means you don't trust people. It may save you from many mistakes, but not all. Suspicion often leads to trusting only when you absolutely must—and often you must trust the wrong people. Complete cynicism is a burden that we try to relieve, but sometimes, in our hunger to find someone honest, we fall for the better "con artist" or the "big liar."

A score of 10 to 14 means you are selective. You want to believe in life. Sometimes your cynicism is a test of others, to find out whether you are being loved or respected for yourself. As long as you are careful, this is a good way to stay reasonable.

You can be happy with a score of 6 to 9 because you believe in the basic goodness of most people. However, unless you are lucky, you may be really hurt. As a basic attitude, trust can oblige other people to respond with trust. If everybody did, it would be wonderful; unfortunately, they do not.

Are "Appearances" Important to You?

For some people, keeping up with the Joneses has become a full-time preoccupation. Why? Often it's because appearances are more important than we care to admit. What about you? Are you more concerned about the impression you are going to make than you really ought to be? You may be convinced that you don't worry too much about the façade. Find out what your real tendencies are.

●

1. You are invited to a party. The people there are dressed much better than you. What are your most likely reactions?

    ☐ a. I feel very uncomfortable. I should have inquired before to find out what other people would be wearing.
    ☐ b. I don't think anybody really noticed my outfit. It was probably only my own feeling that bothered me.
    ☐ c. I like to be comfortable. I don't see why I should conform to others. My clothes were suited to my taste and my personality.

2. You are meeting someone for the first time at a party. He is fairly well known, but you are not. He asks you within a few minutes how much money you are making. What is your reaction?

    ☐ a. He is an important person. I guess he is accustomed to ask direct questions. Probably did not mean any harm.
    ☐ b. No manners, no matter what his position. My income is none of his business. I would give him an evasive answer.
    ☐ c. If I had the guts I would tell him off.

3. A new book is being discussed. Everybody but you seems to have read it. What are you most likely to do?

☐ a. Pretend I've read it too.
☐ b. Say I was just about to read it, but discuss it anyway, based on what I've heard about it.
☐ c. Admit I have not read it and listen to the discussion. Make a note to get it and read it.

4. It's a hot day in the city and hotter in the office and stores. A man in your office wears only an undershirt. What is your reaction?

☐ a. That's carrying it too far; he has no manners.
☐ b. It's okay with me. He has a right to dress the way he likes.
☐ c. I might do the same in his place.

5. A busy executive is explaining a point to his board of directors. He is pointing to a chart while talking.

☐ a. The props are impressive, give him a good buildup.
☐ b. He needs such devices to keep track of things.
☐ c. His props tell the story, save him some thinking.

6. You have to pick up an important person or relative from the airport. You own only a rather shabby old car. What will you do?

☐ a. Drive your own car.
☐ b. Use your car but apologize profusely and tell him your big or better-looking car broke down.
☐ c. Rent an expensive car and pick him/her up with it.

Please turn the page to find out your score and what it means

SCORING

1. a = 3	2. a = 3	3. a = 3
b = 2	b = 2	b = 2
c = 1	c = 1	c = 1
4. a = 3	5. a = 3	6. a = 1
b = 2	b = 2	b = 2
c = 1	c = 1	c = 3

If your score is between 15 and 18, you are usually quite concerned with the impression you make on other people.

A score of 10 to 14 indicates you attach less importance to outward appearances, especially dress or etiquette. Once in a while, though, you are willing to give in to such rules to make a good impression.

A score of 6 to 9 shows you to be someone who doesn't worry too much about what other people think. It could be either a sort of defiance or a real conviction that you don't have to cater to anybody.

Do You Really Know Your Partner? *(for women only)*

One of the most frequent complaints people have about their relationships is that they are not understood by their partners. Sometimes this is due to a lack of meaningful communication, sometimes to a failure to really take time to find out, sometimes a combination of both.

It is very often interesting (and revealing) to gauge the behavior of your partner in various situations and then let him gauge himself in the same way. This "test" holds up a kind of "psychological mirror" to both partners.

You may find that you agree on what type of man he is. Or just the opposite may happen. Sometimes, for example, a woman complains that her man is not decisive enough—he has trouble making up his mind. He in turn feels that the opposite is true.

Such discrepancies do not necessarily have to be only negative. A woman may feel that her husband or lover is very self-assured, whereas he is convinced that he is insecure in many of his daily activities.

Often people fail to ask themselves, when they establish a close relationship, whether or not they really know what they are letting themselves in for. Have they mistaken surface attitudes for real ones in both a negative and a positive sense?

Try, therefore, as honestly as you can to visualize your partner in different types of situations. If you can't think for the moment how he really does behave, you may want to observe him or actually bring about such situations and use them as a kind of three-dimensional "reality" test. This quiz will be particularly interesting and valuable if you let your partner answer the same questions himself, without seeing your answers.

There are no "right" or "wrong" answers. Try to remember that you are not sitting in judgment on your partner. Rather, this test is designed to evaluate how well you know him and how closely your perceptions of him and his perceptions of himself match. It takes courage to be honest. But this quiz is only valuable if you and your partner have that courage.

●

How to Take the Test

1. Take this test when you are relaxed and in a good mood—this applies to your partner as well—otherwise you or he may be negatively influenced.

2. Read each question carefully. Take your time.

3. Write the letter that most closely corresponds to your answer under the column headed YOU.

4. Cover your own answers.

5. Give the quiz to your partner. Have him fill in his answers under the column headed HE.

	HE	YOU
1. He is at a party and another guest, who has had a couple of drinks, says, "You are a bastard!" Would he:	_____	_____
a. say something equally nasty		
b. laugh		
c. ignore it		

	HE	YOU
2. The two of you have been waiting in line for half an hour at the movie box office when a couple barges in line ahead of you. Would he:	_____	_____
a. tell them to go to the back of the line		
b. inform the manager		
c. complain bitterly to the person behind him		

	HE	YOU
3. He is sitting in a crowded bus and gets up to offer his seat to a lady. Suddenly another man jumps into the empty seat. Would he:	_____	_____

      a. grab him and lift him out of the
         seat
      b. walk away disgusted
      c. explain to him that the seat was
         meant for the lady

                                                          HE   YOU

4. You feel very sexy and it shows. Would   _____   _____
   he:
      a. kid you and then comply
      b. feel "funny" and find an excuse
      c. feel flattered and let you seduce
         him

                                                          HE   YOU

5. He is riding in a taxi when the driver
   begins to make derogatory remarks
   about his particular religious group.
   Would he: _____   _____
      a. try to convince the cabbie that
         his prejudices are unfounded
      b. tell him to stop and get out
         without paying the fare
      c. remain silent and consider with-
         holding the tip

                                                          HE   YOU

6. At a dinner party with several other
   couples, someone asks your partner to
   tell a particularly "dirty" joke. He re-
   plies that it is not suitable in mixed
   company. A chorus of "you're too old-
   fashioned" greets his reply. Would he: _____   _____
      a. tell it
      b. insist that the joke is not
         appropriate
      c. offer some excuse for not telling
         it like having forgotten the
         punch line

	HE	YOU

7. He is with a client who takes him, unexpectedly, into a homosexual nightclub. Would he:
    a. try to cajole him into leaving
    b. shut up and suffer
    c. relax and enjoy it

	HE	YOU

8. In decorating the walls of his office, would he choose:
    a. sexy pictures
    b. photographs of the family
    c. paintings

	HE	YOU

9. The two of you are at a party with some close friends. Someone suggests it might be fun to try "group" sex. Would he:
    a. express his feelings on the subject
    b. go along with the group decision
    c. try to gauge your reactions

	HE	YOU

10. If a loved one were afflicted with terminal cancer, would he:
    a. instruct the doctor to tell the person
    b. decide not to tell the person at all
    c. tell the person himself

	HE	YOU

11. You arrive at a cocktail party full of strangers. Would he:
    a. strike up a conversation with an interesting-looking person
    b. head for the drinks

    c. wait for the others to introduce themselves to him

	HE	YOU
12. If he had a year's leave of absence with pay, which would he rather do?	_____	_____

    a. travel abroad
    b. write a novel
    c. attend a university to further his education

	HE	YOU
13. If people suddenly began staring in his direction, would he:	_____	_____

    a. wonder what they are staring at
    b. think there must be something wrong with him
    c. turn to see what was behind him

	HE	YOU
14. Someone begins to make sexual advances to you at a party. Would he, when noticing it:	_____	_____

    a. not pay any attention
    b. accuse you of "asking for it"
    c. joke about your sexiness

	HE	YOU
15. You are alone with him and he wants you, but you don't feel like it. Would he:	_____	_____

    a. insist and try to get his way
    b. give up and accept your reasons
    c. gently try to get you in the right mood

	HE	YOU
16. What he likes *best* about you is:	_____	_____

    a. your brains
    b. your body
    c. your personality

	HE	YOU

17. He thinks your best facial feature is:
    a. your eyes
    b. your mouth and lips
    c. your complexion
	_____	_____

	HE	YOU

18. During an intimate moment, you share with him a past involvement that ended unhappily. Would he:
    a. quickly change the subject
    b. encourage you to talk it out
    c. tell you about one of his previous romances
	_____	_____

Please turn the page to find out your score and what it means

SCORING

1. Check your answers against his.
2. Each time your answers match, score 1 point. Each time they do not match, score 0. The highest possible score is 18—if your answers match for every question.
3. If you score between 15 and 18: Excellent. You know him very well indeed.
4. If you score between 11 and 14: Good. You possess an adequate level of understanding and knowledge.
5. If you score between 6 and 10: Fair. Better knowledge and understanding would seem desirable, or your relationship may not be able to grow.
6. If your score between 0 and 5: Poor. You must make a real effort to develop better understanding and more insight. You may be deliberately "fooling" yourself about him—either over- or underestimating him to make him conform to your image of him.

Regardless of your score, a great deal depends on whether the agreement (or disagreement) is primarily on negative or positive types of reaction. For instance, take 1. If you feel he would answer back in an equally nasty way and he feels the same, it shows that you know him quite well and he too has a pretty good understanding of his bad points. If, on the other hand, you feel he would ignore it and he feels he would answer back in a nasty way, it shows you have a better opinion of him than he has of himself. And so on.

Do You Really Know Your Partner? *(for men only)*

One of the most frequent complaints people have about their relationships is that they are not understood by their partners. Sometimes this is due to a lack of meaningful communication, sometimes to a failure to really take time to find out, sometimes a combination of both.

It is very often interesting (and revealing) to gauge the behavior of your partner in various situations and then let her gauge herself in the same way. This "test" holds up a kind of "psychological mirror" to both partners.

You may find that you and she agree on what type of woman she is. Or just the opposite may happen. Sometimes, for example, a man complains that his wife or lover is not decisive enough—she has trouble making up her mind. She in turn feels that the opposite is true.

Such discrepancies do not necessarily have to be only negative. A man may feel that his wife or lover is very self-assured, whereas she is convinced that she is insecure in many of her daily activities.

Often people fail to ask themselves, when they establish a close relationship, whether or not they really know what they are letting themselves in for. Have they mistaken surface attitudes for real ones in both a negative and a positive sense?

Try, therefore, as honestly as you can to visualize your partner in different types of situations. If you can't think for the moment how she really does behave, you may want to observe her or actually bring about such situations and use them as a kind of three-dimensional "reality" test. This quiz will be particularly interesting and valuable if you let your partner answer the same questions herself, without seeing your answers.

There are no "right" or "wrong" answers. Try to remember that you are not sitting in judgment on your partner. Rather, this test is designed to evaluate how well you know her and how closely your perceptions of her and her perceptions of herself match. It takes courage to be honest. But this quiz is only valuable if you and your partner have that courage.

●

How to Take the Test

1. Take this test when you are relaxed and in a good mood—this applies to your partner as well—otherwise you or she may be negatively influenced.

2. Read each question carefully. Take your time.

3. Write the letter that most closely corresponds to your answer under the column headed YOU.

4. Cover your own answers.

5. Give the quiz to your partner. Have her fill in her answers under the column headed SHE.

	SHE	YOU
1. Somebody is making obvious advances to her. What would she do?	_____	_____

    a. Refuse and get indignant; possibly slap him.
    b. Flirt and play along.
    c. Consider the possibility seriously.

	SHE	YOU
2. You hear that a friend of yours is in financial trouble. He could be helped out with a reasonable amount of money. You are not in favor of doing it. What would your partner do?	_____	_____

    a. Do it on her own and tell you about it afterward.
    b. Discuss it with you and try to convince you to help him after all.
    c. Agree with you not to help this friend, possibly because she feels the two of you need the money more.

3. You are going on a trip with your partner. When you arrive, you discover that something important has been left behind. What would she do?

SHE _____   YOU _____

    a. Blame you, telling you that it is a man's job to arrange trips.

    b. Blame herself for her negligence.

    c. Blame neither one of you; figure out with you how the situation could be remedied.

4. You bought a new car without telling your partner. What will be her reaction?

SHE _____   YOU _____

    a. Tell you if you felt like doing it it was all right with her.

    b. Feel upset about the sudden expenditure and be annoyed.

    c. Tell you that she would not have objected had you told her.

5. At a party, you are trying to find an interesting woman besides your wife to talk with or flirt with. What would she do?

SHE _____   YOU _____

    a. Try to cut in and prevent you from getting too involved.

    b. Leave you alone and kid you afterward.

    c. Compliment you on your "conquest."

6. You want to make love to your partner, but you don't "perform" too well. What is her most likely reaction?

SHE _____   YOU _____

a. Laugh at you and say something like "Getting old?"
b. Try to arouse you by suggesting a different position.
c. Reassure you and say, "You are tired. We'll try again, don't worry."

	SHE	YOU
7. You have gotten a small raise. What is her reaction when you tell her?	_____	_____

    a. She's delighted and shows it.
    b. Complains that it isn't more of a raise.
    c. Sympathizes that it wasn't a large raise, but points out that it *was* something.

	SHE	YOU
8. You are overloaded with work, some of which could be handled by your partner. What is she most likely to do?	_____	_____

    a. Say nothing and leave you alone until you have finished your work.
    b. Ask whether she can help in any way.
    c. Commiserate with you, telling you you shouldn't work so hard, without offering to help.

	SHE	YOU
9. Someone is very rude to your partner and insults her. What would she do?	_____	_____

    a. Strike back, at least verbally, and defend herself quite adequately.

b. Ask you to help defend her, but do her share in the meantime.

c. Be helpless, and cry.

	SHE	YOU

10. She arrives at a gathering and discovers she is either overdressed or not properly dressed. What does she do?   _____   _____

a. Tries to be as inconspicuous as possible, but obviously feels uncomfortable.

b. Makes some remarks about her inappropriate dress.

c. It would not bother her one bit.

	SHE	YOU

11. Your partner has been asked to take a job that will require her being away from you and your home quite often. Your children are all in school. What do you think she will do?   _____   _____

a. She will take the opportunity, pointing out that there will always be time for you and her to be together.

b. She will refuse. Her home and you are more important.

c. She will try to find a compromise.

	SHE	YOU

12. She thinks your best feature is: _____   _____

a. Your eyes.

b. Your hair.

c. Your shoulders.

	SHE	YOU

13. You are invited to an important party, which will probably be very boring. You want your partner to go along. What will she do?   _____   _____

a. Go along even though she knows she will be bored.

b. Try to get you to cancel or go only for a short time.

c. Refuse to go along. It is *your* party and your problem.

	SHE	YOU
14. What would you say your partner likes best about you?	_____	_____

    a. Your brains.

    b. Your ability as a breadwinner.

    c. Your warmth.

	SHE	YOU
15. You feel very sexy, but she is obviously tired and not in the mood. What is she most likely to do?	_____	_____

    a. She will cooperate or try to please you, anyway.

    b. She will suggest waiting until tomorrow.

    c. She will simply refuse and be annoyed at you for being selfish.

	SHE	YOU
16. Your tastes differ as far as the interior decorating of your home is concerned. What is most likely going to happen?	_____	_____

    a. Your taste will prevail.

    b. You will compromise in various areas.

    c. Her taste will prevail.

	SHE	YOU
17. You tell your partner you want to give up your job and get out of the rat race. It will mean a smaller income and a more restricted life. How will she react?	_____	_____

a. She will say, "If it makes you happy, it's fine with me."
b. She will threaten to leave.
c. She will suggest that you not burn all your bridges at once. She might remind you of other ideas of yours that sounded good but didn't quite work out.

	SHE	YOU

18. The doctor told you that you ought to take it easy. Some of your symptoms may be due to stress. What is her reaction likely to be?
    a. She will agree with the doctor, and will help you.
    b. She will be annoyed, and point out that she too is working hard.
    c. She will suggest that your symptoms are more psychological than real.

Please turn the page to find out your score and what it means

SCORING

1. Check your answers against hers.
2. Each time your answers match, score 1 point. Each time they do not match, score 0. The highest possible score is 18—if your answers match for every question.
3. If you score between 15 and 18: Excellent. You know her very well indeed.
4. If you score between 11 and 14: Good. You possess an adequate level of understanding and knowledge.
5. If you score between 6 and 10: Fair. Better knowledge and understanding would seem desirable, or your relationship may not be able to grow.
6. If you score between 0 and 5: Poor. You must make a real effort to develop better understanding and more insight. You may be deliberately "fooling" yourself about her—either over- or underestimating her to make her conform to your image of her.

Regardless of your score, a great deal depends on whether the agreement (or disagreement) is primarily on negative or positive types of reaction.

Are You Jealous of Others?

Jealousy is a struggle between the belief that you are as good as the other person and the fear that you aren't. When an office colleague gets a promotion before you do, when someone has more money or is more successful than you, you begin to doubt yourself.

It is natural to be aware of your competitors. You need to feel that you yourself are reasonably successful. But if you constantly fear the success of others, you are jealous and destructive, rather than friendly and constructive.

What is your own jealousy rating? To find out if you have more than a normal amount of jealousy, study the six situations described below. Then, for each, check the one item that comes closest to your own reaction.

●

1. In an office, two men shake hands while a third man looks on. You interpret this little scene correctly: Joe's idea will be used; Jim, who had a similar idea first, but whose suggestion was rejected, looks on. What will happen?

   ☐ a. Jim is going to make it known that he had the same basic idea first.

   ☐ b. Jim decides to wish Joe good luck, and say nothing about his idea.

   ☐ c. Jim plans to present an even better version of the idea soon.

2. A man and his wife are standing on the sidewalk. The wife is talking to another man. You interpret correctly that Mrs. Smith has met an old beau, and talks to him while her husband waits. What do you think Mr. Smith will do?

☐ a. Mr. Smith is annoyed and explains that he is irritated because of the long delay.

☐ b. Mr. Smith is patient and simply stands by until they finish talking.

☐ c. Mr. Smith tries to join in their conversation as much as possible.

3. Two sisters, Anne and Mary, are sitting next to each other at a party. A man asks Anne to dance. Mary looks annoyed; Anne is always being asked to dance, while her sister often sits out. What is your reaction?

☐ a. Anne deserves to be popular; she's much brighter and more agreeable.

☐ b. Mary has many other interests; she doesn't really care for dancing.

☐ c. Anne pushes herself forward; no wonder she's so much more successful.

4. You are discussing your stock-market investments with a friend. He boasts, telling you how he sold all his stocks before the market went down, and didn't lose a penny. What is your reaction?

☐ a. He is probably lying. Everybody makes wrong investments once in a while.

☐ b. Maybe I just am not smart enough. I could have foreseen the same things he did.

☐ c. I did not do as badly as all that. I exaggerate a little to others, too.

5. You are on your way home from a party at the beautiful home of your friends. You discuss your friends' home. What are you most likely to say?

☐ a. It must have cost a pretty penny. I'd like to see their oil bill and their taxes.

☐ b. If they can afford it, why not? I'd do the same thing. Someday I might.

☐ c. So our house is smaller and less elegant, but it suits me fine.

6. You hear about the success of a relative in either the music, literary, or business field. What is your reaction?

- ☐ a. We have the same genes, same family. Why did *he* make it? Must be a fluke.
- ☐ b. He or she worked hard. I am proud to be related to him.
- ☐ c. I am happy. I have my own strong points. Who needs to be famous?

Please turn the page to find out your score and what it means

SCORING

Add your score according to the following key:

1. a = 3	2. a = 3	3. a = 1
b = 2	b = 1	b = 2
c = 1	c = 2	c = 3
4. a = 3	5. a = 3	6. a = 3
b = 2	b = 1	b = 1
c = 1	c = 2	c = 2

If you scored between 16 and 18, you are extremely jealous of others. You might want to work on it, since you're probably hurting yourself much more than you're hurting others.

A score of 10 to 15 is a good average. You are capable of enjoying somebody else's success and strengths, increasing your own value in doing it.

A score of 6 to 9 indicates a strong feeling of satisfaction with oneself. Maybe you are less than ambitious—or perhaps you have attained your goals and have no real reason to be jealous.

Do You Try to Be the Most Important Person in Any Group?

Some of us are happiest if we are inconspicuous, don't have to say much, and don't have to perform. Others seem almost automatically to dominate a group, become leaders, talk more than others, and seem to know all the answers. More often than not, the role each of us plays in any group is something we choose, consciously or unconsciously.

The following quiz may help you discover which choice you tend to make. Once you're aware of it, you may want to change.

As you look at each situation, try to remember how you reacted in a similar one. Then check the appropriate response for you.

●

1. You are at a dinner party with some friends and some strangers. There is a lively discussion of a topic such as art or politics.

   - ☐ a. I just listen most of the time.
   - ☐ b. I quickly dominate the discussion.
   - ☒ c. I participate when I have something to say.

2. You have just listened to a lecture. There is a question-and-answer session afterward. What is your usual behavior?

   - ☐ a. I wait until several people have asked questions.
   - ☐ b. I am usually the one to open the discussion.
   - ☒ c. I prefer to listen to everybody.

3. You are in a car with four or five other people. You are searching for a restaurant, but the driver seems to be lost. What do you do?

   - ☐ a. I give directions, get out a map, or indicate landmarks.
   - ☒ b. I listen to opinions of others and make *my* suggestions.
   - ☐ c. It is not my problem. Let the driver find the restaurant.

4. At a business meeting with your two partners, a decision has to made about future plans. What do you do?

☐ a. I usually keep silent, unless asked.
☐ b. I quickly take the leadership.
☒ c. When I see the others fumble, I take over.

5. We are in a sightseeing bus. Departure was set for 9 A.M. It is now 9:30.

☒ a. I complain to my neighbors in the bus.
☐ b. I get up to find out what's going on and protest the delay.
☐ c. I wait. There is probably a good reason. No sense getting all excited.

6. A dangerous fire starts and spreads in your apartment house. Everybody is panicky and confused.

☐ a. I would become panicky, too.
☒ b. I would immediately organize a calm exit and escape.
☐ c. I would suggest that someone take the lead and get things going in order to save everybody.

Please turn the page to find out your score and what it means

SCORING

Add your score according to the following key:

1. a = 1	2. a = 2	3. a = 3
b = 3	b = 3	b = 2
c = 2	c = 1	c = 1
4. a = 1	5. a = 2	6. a = 1
b = 3	b = 3	b = 3
c = 2	c = 1	c = 2

A score of 15 to 18 shows that you usually try to take the lead or to be the most important person in any given group.

10-14 puts you into the category of people who do not try to dominate, but can help and get things going if they are needed.

6-9 indicates a preference for a more passive role. You don't usually feel adequate or comfortable in an exposed position.

None of these roles is "right" or "wrong." Sometimes we train ourselves to become leaders because it's the only position in which we feel we can function. Of course, there are people who thrust themselves into an important role without being qualified for it. Their discomfort usually shows quickly. In order to be an important person in a group you need the consent of the group.

Sometimes it can be interesting to try to get out of a passive role. You may discover that you have qualities for an important role without having realized it.

Are You a Good Parent?

Should you be firm or give in, be permissive or be a disciplinarian? The kind of parent you are often depends on your own upbringing, experience, and awareness of yourself.

A child's main job is growing up. Where he stands, it's a world full of knees. People are big, things are hard to reach, and even buttoning a shirt or tying a shoe is a major problem.

If you as an adult can put yourself down on a two-foot-six level, you can at least partially understand your child's struggle to live in the world at the same time he is learning to live in it. He wants and needs security and love; but he also wants and needs to stand on his own feet.

How are ordinary human parents supposed to cope with him? How can they love and protect a child—and at the same time let him develop his own sense of responsibility and independence?

The long climb from childhood to maturity is full of bumps and spills. One day Johnny wants to dress himself; the next day he refuses even to put on his socks. One morning Susie behaves like a "little lady"; that night she says she is afraid to go to bed in a dark room. The twins go at clay modeling like two quiet angels—but they also put up a joint howl at the prospect of having their ears washed.

Beneath these seeming contradictions is a child's struggle between his desire to grow up and his inability to do it easily. It's a hard job, and he knows it.

Parents cannot protect a child from all the hard knocks, but patience and understanding will help a lot. To see how you rate as a parent, study the situations below. For each one, check the statement that best describes your own reaction.

●

1. You walk past the door of your child's room. She is obviously struggling to button her blouse.

☐ a. I want to button it for her; she's really just a baby.
☐ b. I'll let her do it herself; she might as well learn now as any time.
☒ c. I'll show her how, and then perhaps it will be easier for her next time.

2. You are sitting in the living room, reading the papers. Your son comes in and asks you to play with him.

☐ a. He ought to know better than to interrupt.
☐ b. I'll play for a while, then explain why I must go back to my reading.
☒ c. I'll put my paper aside, and play as long as he wants to.

3. You've been painting the house, and you left the ladder up. After lunch you go outside and find your eight-year-old daughter climbing the ladder.

☐ a. I'll order that child to get down at once—she needs a good scolding.
☐ b. I'll let her alone. She looks sure-footed enough to take care of herself.
☒ c. I'll explain why people must be careful, and help her get down.

4. You find your little boy curled up on his bed, crying.

☐ a. I just want to take him in my arms, hold him tight, and cuddle him.
☐ b. I'll tell him to forget it and stop—that big boys just don't cry.
☒ c. I'll pick him up, talk to him, and find out why he is crying.

5. You and your spouse are having a fight. Your children come in from the backyard and wonder what's happening.

☐ a. It won't hurt them to learn to face realities.

☑ b. You explain that grownups fight just as children do. As long as they make up, it is all right.

☐ c. You are embarrassed when you notice how upset they are over your fight. You tell them to go to their rooms.

6. Dad tells the children that he is too busy to go on the picnic they had planned. The family will stay home. Mom disagrees and suggests they go after all.

☐ a. Mom and Dad have a right to have different opinions. Dad has the authority and should be obeyed.

☑ b. The children should also be asked; a vote should be taken by all family members.

☐ c. Dad should stay home, and Mom take the kids to the picnic.

Please turn the page to find out your score and what it means

SCORING

Add your scores according to the following key:

1. a = 1	2. a = 1	3. a = 1
b = 2	b = 2	b = 2
c = 3	c = 3	c = 3
4. a = 2	5. a = 2	6. a = 1
b = 1	b = 3	b = 3
c = 3	c = 1	c = 2

A score of 16 to 18 shows that you try to understand your children and treat them as people as often as you can. You use your authority only to teach them to help themselves and to learn to grow up more easily.

10-15 probably indicates a combination of trying to be helpful and protective, on the one hand, and being a disciplinarian, on the other.

6-9: You are probably a bit too harsh, using your "rank" as a parent a bit too often. Some discipline, of course, is necessary to give children a feeling of security; but it should always be combined with the development of insight and self-motivation.

How Liberated Are You? *(for women)*

You've come a long way, baby. But how far, really? Some women who consider themselves liberated still find it very difficult to give up many of the "privileges" of being "a lady" when "a gentleman" is around. Others scorn these customs, believing they are not privileges, but outmoded ways for men to be nice about showing who's really boss.

Where do you fit in?

●

1. You are riding in a car driven by a man. When you arrive at your destination and he stops the car, what do you do?

   ☐ a. I wait until he comes around to open the door for me.
   ☒ b. I open the door myself.
   ☐ c. I remind him silently of his duty as a gentleman by a look or a gesture.

2. When going to a restaurant, other than with my husband or long-time boyfriend,

   ☐ a. I insist on going Dutch.
   ☐ b. I pay for myself if I can afford it better than he can.
   ☒ c. I expect the man to pay and let him.

3. Think of homemaking duties, like laundry, cooking, and dishwashing. What is the practice in your house?

   ☒ a. My husband does the laundry (or dishes or cooking) quite regularly, or helps me.
   ☐ b. I would not let him do it. He would resent it.
   ☐ c. I let him cook or do the dishes if he enjoys it, but would not insist.

4. Consider investments, buying stock, taking care of the mortgage or savings book. Which of the following comes closest to your attitude?

- [ ] a. A man knows more about these things. At least mine does. He takes care of important financial things.
- [ ] b. We share and discuss most such problems and are partners.
- [ ] c. I have more patience and am more cautious about financial matters. It has nothing to do with being a woman.

5. You hear a couple exchanging insults. Which of the two, man or woman, would you side with instinctively?

- [ ] a. The man.
- [ ] b. Neither; I'd try to arbitrate.
- [ ] c. The woman.

6. You hear about a woman who made it to the top because she slept with her boss. Your honest reaction, please?

- [ ] a. Good for her. Why not use it if you've got it!
- [ ] b. If it seemed to be the only way to get ahead, maybe she was being realistic.
- [ ] c. That route is never worth it. What kind of "success" does anyone get that way?

Please turn the page to find out your score and what it means

SCORING

Add your score according to the following key:

1. a = 1	2. a = 3	3. a = 3
b = 3	b = 2	b = 1
c = 2	c = 1	c = 2
4. a = 1	5. a = 1	6. a = 1
b = 3	b = 2	b = 2
c = 2	c = 3	c = 3

A score of 16 to 18 shows that you carry your "liberation" even into your daily relations with men. When you *think* liberation, you also *act* it.

10-15 is a medium score. In which areas do you still feel you act or want to be treated according to a traditional role? You may want to change your attitudes. Or perhaps not.

6-9 shows that you are still more comfortable in the traditional role. If you feel more comfortable with this role, stick with it. But try to be tolerant of other women's attitudes. Those women too may have a point.

How Liberated Are You? *(for men)*

Women's lib has offered challenges and opportunities to men. For example, they do not necessarily have to be the only breadwinners in the family. In divorce cases, alimony may not have to be paid.

The psychological consequences of men's lib are often more difficult to accept. Many men have to learn new roles. You may accept woman's complete equality as a person, but to what extent has it liberated you as a male?

The following test attempts to help you to ascertain your degree of real liberation.

•

1. While making love, your female partner requests or suggests a position usually reserved for men. What is your reaction?

   ☐ a. Should be fun.
   ☐ b. I would feel uncomfortable, but I guess I would try it.
   ☐ c. I don't think I could perform.

2. Your partner makes more money than you do. How do you feel about it?

   ☐ a. Makes life easier for me.
   ☐ b. I would resent it sooner or later.
   ☐ c. I would try to compete with her.

3. In a restaurant your female partner settles the bill and decides on the tip. What is your reaction?

   ☐ a. I would feel embarrassed in front of the waiter or friends.
   ☐ b. I don't like to bother with such things. I am glad to be with an independent woman.
   ☐ c. I would prefer if she checked the bill but let me sign or pay.

4. Your wife does most of the driving in your family car.

   ☐ a. O.K. by me. I can relax.
   ☐ b. I feel I can handle a car better, particularly on a long trip.
   ☐ c. Would prefer sharing the driving.

5. Your children are having problems in school. The teacher asks the parents to come in. Should your wife handle the situation alone?

   ☐ a. I would not let her do it alone. As a father, I share that job.
   ☐ b. Of course. She's responsible for the children during the day.
   ☐ c. I would prefer it if she asks me first for advice.

6. Your female partner asks you to sew on your own buttons, stitch something, or do the wash. What is your reaction?

   ☐ a. She is trying to humiliate me.
   ☐ b. If I can do it, I will, and I think I can.
   ☐ c. I might have fun doing it a few times, but not as a steady diet.

Please turn the page to find out your score and what it means

SCORING

Add your scores according to the following key:

1. a = 3	2. a = 3	3. a = 2
b = 2	b = 2	b = 3
c = 1	c = 1	c = 1
4. a = 3	5. a = 3	6. a = 1
b = 1	b = 1	b = 3
c = 2	c = 2	c = 2

If your score is between 15 and 18, you are secure as a man and do not feel threatened by reversing roles.

10-14: You are partially liberated. The significance of the score depends on whether or not the situation represents a more radical threat to your accustomed superior role, as in questions 2, 3, or 1, or whether it is less significant, as in 5 or 4.

A score of 6 to 9 reveals discomfort with changes in your role. In most instances you prefer to perpetuate the customary role of the man. How do you think you would score on this test in ten years?

How Observant Are You Really?

By observing others and yourself carefully, you can often decipher hidden communications. Gestures often say more than words. Someone may fold his arms simply because he is cold, or because the position is restful; on the other hand, such a gesture may be indicative of a hidden personality trait. Kicking or swinging a leg may indicate impatience.

To find out what mannerisms mean, take the test below. Give yourself 2 points for each gesture you use *often,* 1 point if you do it *sometimes,* and 0 if you *never* do it. Score yourself fairly and then read the explanations below.

You can use the same test to observe others whom you meet often. Watching them carefully, you can discover many useful things about them and yourself.

●

1. *Doodling*
   Often _____
   Sometimes ___X___
   Never _____

2. *Rubbing chin*
   Often _____
   Sometimes _____
   Never ___X___

3. *Holding cigarette or pen or pencil tightly*
   Often _____
   Sometimes _____
   Never ___X___

4. *Biting fingernails*
   Often _____
   Sometimes _____
   Never ___X___

5. *Caressing leg*
   Often _____
   Sometimes _____
   Never ___X___

6. *Gritting teeth*
   Often _____
   Sometimes _____
   Never ___X___

7. *Stretching*
   Often _____
   Sometimes __✗__
   Never _____

8. *Pulling ear*
   Often _____
   Sometimes _____
   Never __✗__

9. *Not finishing cigarette*
   (if you smoke)
   Often _____
   Sometimes _____
   Never __⊘__

10. *Twirling strand of*
    hair or beard
    Often _____
    Sometimes _____
    Never __✗__

11. *Clenching fingers*
    Often _____
    Sometimes _____
    Never __✗__

12. *Drumming fingers*
    Often _____
    Sometimes _____
    Never __✗__

13. *Raising eyebrows*
    Often _____
    Sometimes __✗__
    Never _____

14. *Folding arms*
    Often _____
    Sometimes __✗__
    Never _____

15. *Covering mouth*
    Often _____
    Sometimes __✗__
    Never _____

Please turn the page to find out your score and what it means

SCORING

If you scored as low as 0 to 5, you are very restrained; it may be due to your excellent verbal means of expression, or to a strong suppression of outward signs of your inner thoughts.

A score of 6 to 13 indicates more flexibility. You don't hold back as much; you use a fair number of expressive gestures.

A score of 14 to 21 indicates a pretty even balance between your verbal and gestural expressiveness.

If you scored between 22 and 30, you are on the extreme side. You either cover up a lot of verbal shortcomings with mannerisms, or you are so rich in thoughts that language alone can't suffice.

As is sometimes the case with extremes, if you are in the low 0-5 or high 22-30 group, your pattern of mannerisms can be read two ways. You will have to examine your psychological reactions and decide which of the two applies in your case.

Mannerisms are a kind of sign language. A psychologist doesn't depend on words alone to learn what another person is thinking. He may find an important clue in a simple habit like doodling. He uses such a clue to help him understand both himself and others. You, too, can develop this sixth sense.

Frequently, doodling indicates a tendency to think structurally and visually. It may also simply serve as an activity outlet for your energies when you are forced to sit still.

Rubbing your chin, pulling your ear, caressing your leg, twirling a strand of hair, folding your arms, clenching your fingers, all establish closer contact with your own self. If you do many of these things often, it may show that you do not feel sure of yourself.

Holding a cigarette stiffly can be interpreted as an attempt to keep people at a distance. Not finishing cigarettes shows nervousness and impatience, as well as a desire to shorten the interval before lighting a new one.

Fingernail biting, like gum chewing, produces saliva and imitates eating. Practiced frequently, it shows a need for reassurance.

Gritting your teeth, if a real habit, expresses aggressiveness and determination. Drumming your fingers is a primitive form of hypnotism; if you do it often, you may be very assertive. Stretching, too, is a preliminary step toward action. It makes you feel awake and ready to meet the situation.

Covering your mouth while talking may be a sign of timidity. On the other hand, the person who raises his eyebrows may be trying to show responsive, open interest.

You can't take any of these interpretations as absolute, for circumstances may change a meaning. But you can be sure that the language of gestures is a real and revealing one. Next time you see a movie, watch for a scene where the crushing-out of a cigarette, for example, is more expressive than several dramatic lines.

Are You the Kind of Person Who Should Be Married?

Bachelors of both sexes have long had to defend themselves against the attempts of their friends and families to marry them off. Almost every single woman over the age of twenty is apt to feel vaguely or acutely guilty about her single state. Men, much less so. Society still tends to think that every girl "ought" to be married, and that if she isn't, she is not fulfilling herself as a woman.

Actually, there are some men and women who would probably be happier if they never married. Then there are men and women who may someday marry happily and well, but who, for now, bide their time.

Which type are you? Take our quiz and see. In each of the six categories below, check the one statement that best represents your point of view. Then give the same quiz to your partner and see how your answers compare.

●

1. *Furniture*

   ☒ a. The husband and wife should decide together on the furniture and décor; otherwise neither will be happy.
   ☐ b. A wife/husband should rely on her husband's/his wife's judgment about such a major purchase.
   ☐ c. A man or woman should not give up his or her ideas on how the home should look just because they disagree. One or the other should have her/his way.

2. *Food*

   ☐ a. A woman should usually serve a man's favorite dishes.
   ☐ b. The wife should decide what to serve.
   ☒ c. Many men are excellent cooks; husband and wife could plan the meals together.

3. *Children*

☐ a. Society should not expect you to have children if you do not really want them.

☒ b. A couple should not have children until they are both ready for them.

☐ c. It is important for a man to have a son to carry on the family name.

4. *Sex*

☐ a. A woman should be receptive to a man's sexual needs. Her sex drive is less insistent than his.

☐ b. She should be able to say yes or no, depending on her mood.

☒ c. A woman should express her sexual needs as openly as a man.

5. *At a party*

☒ a. A husband and wife should circulate together to meet other people. They are a couple and belong together.

☐ b. The wife or the husband should socialize by herself or himself to meet interesting people.

☐ c. When a husband is escorting his wife, he should pay special attention to her needs.

6. *Freedom*

☐ a. Both husband and wife should have freedom to have temporary affairs.

☐ b. A woman should give her husband freedom to "play around" as long as he comes back to her, but not insist on hers.

☒ c. Unless they are "faithful" to each other, they won't have a happy marriage.

Please turn the page to find out your score and what it means

SCORING

Add your six scores according to the following key:

1. a = 3
    b = 2
    c = 1
	2. a = 2
	    b = 1
	    c = 3
		3. a = 1
		    b = 2
		    c = 3

4. a = 1
    b = 2
    c = 3
	5. a = 3
	    b = 1
	    c = 2
		6. a = 1
		    b = 2
		    c = 3

If your score was 6 to 9, you are probably too independent to be happy in any marriage or long-term relationship. Though you may be strongly attracted to someone else, you will soon find that person's company quite oppressive if it forces you to make changes in your way of life. You are proud of your ability to stand up for yourself and to direct the course of your life without help or interference from anyone. *Your* ideas, *your* desires, *your* way of doing things—more than anyone else's—are what is important to you. Sometimes you may appear selfish as a result, but actually you can be a very generous person as long as you don't feel your liberties are being encroached upon.

If you scored between 10 and 14, you're an "ideal bachelor." You like being single and you feel no desire to rush into marriage. You can easily have a long-term affair in which both partners are as much friends as lovers. You can also handle two, three, or more relationships without ever losing your cool. When and if you do marry, it should be someone who can respect your need to be private—someone just as independent as you are.

If your score was 15 to 18, when you get married you'll share everything. You not only believe in equality between the sexes, you practice it. As equal partners in the marriage, you will probably both have jobs—even though one of you may not need to work—and you will expect your partner to do a fair share of the housework. The ideal mate for you is someone from your own crowd, someone who has the same interests, ideas, hobbies, and friends as you do.

How Sensuous Are You?

You have five senses. Do you always use them? Some of us are visually oriented; others use the sense of touch more often. Some people can smell a subtle spice in food; others don't even notice garlic. Noise can bother some people and not even be noticed by others.

Sensuousness involves measuring how much you use the antennas nature has given you. What we are interested in is not only how many of your five senses you are using, but how intensely they are being used.

●

1. When I am studying or reading

   ☑ a. I prefer to have background music going.
   ☐ b. I can't concentrate on work if there is noise or music.
   ☐ c. I get accustomed to noise or music if it is repetitious in nature.

2. Can you describe or sketch the roof lines of your neighbor's house or your office building or work place or the view from the window you look out most often?

   ☐ a. Yes, very easily.
   ☐ b. Some of it only.
   ☒ c. I would have to go to look.

3. Close your eyes. Try to recall the odor of places you have been or people you know.

   ☐ a. Can't do it.
   ☐ b. Yes, I can smell 1, 2, 3, 4, 5 different locations or people. (Circle the corresponding number.)
   ☒ c. I would have to go back there or see a picture in order to do it.

4. When you are being served a strange dish, what do you usually do?

- ☒ a. Just eat it to see what it tastes like.
- ☐ b. Push the food around on the plate to see clearly what it is.
- ☐ c. Smell it first on a spoon or fork or by bending down over the plate.

5. What part does your sense of smell play when you are making love?

- ☒ a. I like to smell the perfume, cologne, or just perspiration.
- ☐ b. I prefer love-making to be odorless; smells interfere with my involvement.
- ☐ c. I know how my partner smells and I like it or am accustomed to it.

6. When I make love, I spend time

- ☐ a. touching
- ☒ b. looking
- ☐ c. smelling
- ☐ d. licking
- ☐ e. making sounds, talking, or listening

Assign a number from 1 to 5 for each to indicate how often you use a particular sense (5 indicates "always," whereas 1 indicates "seldom, if ever").

Please turn the page to find out your score and what it means

SCORING

Add your score according to the following key:

1. a = 3
   b = 1
   c = 2

2. a = 3
   b = 2
   c = 1

3. a = 1
   b = 3
   (or 4 if you checked more than 3 locations)
   c = 2

4. a = 1
   b = 2
   c = 3

5. a = 3
   b = 1
   c = 2

6. 5 to 25

The highest score is 30 to 41. You are using all your senses in many situations. You get more out of life. You are probably capable of writing. A person who can observe and use all his sense antennas may well be able to describe those experiences in such a way that others can have a similar experience.

A score of 19 to 29 is a good average. Most of us are sensually alert only some of the time. Remember, we have eyes, ears, noses, and tongues in order to use them.

If you score between 10 and 18, you have a more abstract, less direct approach to your environment. It might be good if you trained your senses more and tried to listen, smell, see, hear, and touch what goes on around you.

How Hostile Are You Compared to Others?

Hidden hostility can be very costly. It can influence your judgment and can antagonize other people, since few of us are good enough actors really to hide these negative feelings. While the quiz that follows is not aimed at helping you to overcome your hostilities, it should make you aware of them. This is usually the first step in helping you either to live with your frustrations and hostilities and accept them consciously or to do something constructive about them.

By taking this test you may learn to observe yourself in a more honest fashion; maybe then you will be better able to free yourself from repressive and potentially harmful feelings of hostility.

Put yourself in the following situations. Then check the response that most nearly approximates what your own response would be.

•

1. You find out that a co-worker left for her vacation pretending that everything was taken care of. Instead, you had to do her work, since it could not wait until her return. What would be your reaction?

   ☐ a. I would be angry, but I would swallow it, and not complain when she got back.
   ☐ b. I would tell her a few days after her return how unfair she had been and ask her to explain.
   ☐ c. I would explode and write to her if I could reach her. I would tell everybody in the office or place of work what a louse she had been.
   ☐ d. I would say nothing, but decide to take revenge at the very first opportunity.

2. A husband forgets his wife's birthday or wedding anniversary. Here is how some people react. Which one do you sympathize with?

☐ a. She laughs and kids about it, but figures that "that's my husband."

☐ b. Says nothing, but is in a bad mood and takes it out in different ways.

☐ c. Discusses her disappointment with her husband.

☐ d. Blows her top when she's sure it was forgotten and makes him pay for his oversight.

☐ e. Tries various tricks to make him remember, but is slightly annoyed that this was necessary.

3. Make a list of people you dislike and try to figure out your reasons. Be honest.

NAMES	*REASONS*
_____	_____
_____	_____
_____	_____
_____	_____
_____	_____
_____	_____
_____	_____
_____	_____
_____	_____

Are you surprised about how many or how few people you dislike, or do you think your list is average?

4. If you had the courage, whom would you: (Fill in a name, then check one of the columns on the right, depending on what your reaction would be, once you had done it.)

	FEEL BETTER	FEEL SORRY
a. Tell off _____	_____	_____
b. Never see again _____	_____	_____
c. Hit_____	_____	_____
d. Spit on _____	_____	_____
e. Kill in your imagination _____	_____	_____

5. A restaurant waiter comes to your table after you have been sitting there for twenty minutes and have made repeated requests. He says, "What's the hurry?" Who, among the following customers, is most like you? The one who . . .

- ☐ a. Says little but is obviously mad and orders in a surly fashion.
- ☐ b. Leaves only a small tip.
- ☐ c. Walks out after having given the waiter a piece of his or her mind.
- ☐ d. Reprimands him and says: "You know I have been sitting here for twenty minutes without any service." If he apologizes, calms down.
- ☐ e. Grumbles about general conditions and submits to waiter's "insults."

6. Think about someone you know and dislike. Suppose that he/she is represented by a potato. What would you do to him/her?

- ☐ a. Bite into it.
- ☐ b. Slice it up.
- ☐ c. Caress it.
- ☐ d. Crush it with a hammer.

7. Which of these people do you feel inferior to?

- [ ] a. Waiters
- [ ] b. Cab drivers
- [ ] c. Policemen
- [ ] d. Teachers
- [ ] e. Doctors
- [ ] f. Lawyers
- [ ] g. Parents
- [ ] h. Brothers
- [ ] i. Sisters

8. Imagine that you are very mad at somebody and that he or she can hurt you. What are you most likely to do?

- [ ] a. Express your anger to this person despite the danger of retaliation.
- [ ] b. Let out your hostility on somebody else who you know cannot hurt you.
- [ ] c. Swallow your anger and just get into a bad mood.

9. Have you ever wished anybody dead among family members, friends, or acquaintances? (This may have shown up only in a dream or a fantasy.) Pick as many as you wish.

- [ ] a. Father
- [ ] b. Mother
- [ ] c. Husband or boyfriend
- [ ] d. Wife
- [ ] e. Business associate
- [ ] f. Boss
- [ ] g. American political leader
- [ ] h. Foreign leader
- [ ] i. Girlfriend

Please turn the page to find out your score and what it means

SCORING

Score yourself according to which answer you chose:

1. a = 2
   b = 1
   c = 2
   d = 3

2. a = 1
   b = 2
   c = 1
   d = 3
   e = 2

3. Give yourself 1 point for each person you dislike and 1 point for each good reason. If you have no reason and still dislike that person, score yourself with 2 points.

4.

	Feel Better	Feel Sorry
a =	1	2
b =	1	2
c =	2	3
d =	2	3
e =	3	2

5. a = 3
   b = 2
   c = 3
   d = 1
   e = 2

6. a = 2
   b = 3
   c = 2
   d = 4

7. a = 2	f = 1	8. a = 2
b = 3	g = 1	b = 3
c = 2	h = 2	c = 4
d = 1	i = 2	
e = 1	none = 0	

9. a = 3	f = 2
b = 4	g = 1
c = 3	h = 1
d = 3	i = 3
e = 2	

If you have between 55 and 75 points, you have a large number of hidden hostilities and have either not been aware of them or do not express them. (We gave you higher scores for those answers in which you swallowed your anger than when you expressed it openly; as, for example, in 8 c.)

A score of 36 to 54 puts you into a less hostile group and indicates that you are a person who lets go, explodes once in a while, but has a normal range of hostilities, as most of us do.

If your score is between 12 and 35, you are indeed very open about your hostilities or have few of them. Those that you do have, you discuss openly and try to resolve and control.

Can You Spot a Problem in Your Love Relationship? *(for men and women)*

How well do you and your partner play your roles in your relationship? Is the play falling apart, losing its excitement? Do you sometimes feel that perhaps the players were miscast?

Feelings of uncertainty and frustration are common among couples who have been married or involved for a while. They even occur between the boyfriend and the girlfriend who have known each other for quite some time.

The big question is, however, Are your feelings of uncertainty and discontent merely part of the normal flow of life or do they indicate that there might be a crack in your relationship?

In order to help you answer this question for your own relationship, we have devised a test, which should be taken first by one partner, then by the other. Basically, the questions on all parts of the test are interchangeable for men and for women; where individual questions require alterations for men or for women, please select the alternative that is appropriate for you (for example: his/her; he/she).

We have listed several areas; in each area, we have defined potential problems and ask you to decide the degree to which this is a problem for you.

Once you have completed the quiz, score yourself and then find out what your scores mean individually and collectively.

●

1. *Conversation piece*

   Let's say you have 100 hours to talk with your partner—100 hours spread out, of course, over a number of days. How much of that time would you spend talking about each of the following topics?

   The list of topics is divided, as you see on the chart below, into four major categories: *your* interests; *your partner's* interests; *necessary, mutual* interests; and *worldly* interests. Under each of the four categories we have also left space for other topics we might not have thought of. If you need the spaces, fill in additional topics. If there are some topics listed that you wouldn't talk about, simply skip them.

   Remember, the total number of hours for the whole chart must not exceed 100.

Yours	Hours
Food, fashion	___
Social life outside this relationship	___
Hobbies	___
Personal problems	___
Job	___
Friends and relatives	___
Money problems	___
_____	___
_____	___
_____	___
_____	___
Total	___

Your partner's	Hours
Food, fashion	___
Social life outside this relationship	___
Hobbies	___
Personal problems	___
Job	___
Friends and relatives	___
Money problems	___
_____	___
_____	___
_____	___
Total	___

Necessary and mutual	Hours
Money problems	___
Travel	___
Sex	___
Plans for future	___
Children	___
Friends and relatives	___
Apartment or house	___
_____	___
_____	___
_____	___
Total	___

Worldly	Hours
Politics	___
Religion	___
World events	___
Art, music, literature	___
Social issues	___
_____	___
_____	___
_____	___
_____	___
_____	___
Total	___

• 189

SCORING FOR 1

Analyzing the number of hours you devote to these topics gives you some idea whether your conversations with each other are balanced or lopsided.

When you have filled in the chart, add the total number of hours spent for each of the four categories and fill in the "Total" blank at the bottom of each category. (Again, be sure the total of all four columns doesn't exceed 100.)

If each of the four areas is 25, score yourself "excellent." Otherwise, score yourself according to the following key: If any of the four areas is: 80 or more or 5 or less—Very Poor; 65 to 79 or 6 to 10—Poor; 50 to 64 or 11 to 15—Below Average; 32 to 49 or 16 to 18—Average; 29 to 31 or 19 to 21—Good; 26 to 28 or 22 to 24—Very Good.

2. *Understanding and being understood*

Do you feel that you understand your partner as a person better, the same, or less well than you did two years ago? Check a, b, or c in the question below. (If you have been married or going together less than two years, do you understand your partner better, the same, or less well than you did six months ago?) Do you feel your partner understands you better, the same, or less well now than before?

I understand my partner.

☐ a. better
☐ b. the same
☐ c. less well

My partner understands me

☐ a. better
☐ b. the same
☐ c. less well

Please turn the page to find out your score and what it means

SCORING FOR 2

The longer you know someone, the better you should understand him/her and the better he/she should understand you. If your two answers are:

Both "better"   *Very good*
One "better," one "the same"   *Good*
Both "the same"   *Below average*
One "well," the other "the same" or "better"   *Poor*
Both "less well"   *Very poor*

3. *Friendship*

In column A below, list friends who really mean something to you. Do not list acquaintances, just friends. In column B, list all of your partner's good friends (not acquaintances).

A   B

_____   _____

_____   _____

_____   _____

_____   _____

_____   _____

_____   _____

_____   _____

_____   _____

_____   _____

Please turn the page to find out your score and what it means

SCORING FOR 3

Many relationships begin to falter when neither party *respects* the other's friends.

If *all* the friends listed in column A and column B are the same, score your relationship "Good."

If *half or slightly more* of the friends listed in columns A and B are the same, score your relationship "Average."

If *less than half* of the friends in columns A and B are the same, score your relationship "Less than adequate" in terms of your mutual friends.

4. *Fantasies*

   a. Suppose you knew that your partner, while waiting in a dentist's or a doctor's office, was deeply engrossed in admiring the centerfold in *Playboy/Playgirl* magazine. What would your reaction be? Check one:
      - ☐ w. Shocked. What a filthy mind!
      - ☐ x. Embarrassed. Other people might see my partner reading such trash.
      - ☒ y. No reaction. It's normal for anyone.
      - ☐ z. Not surprised. Men/Women are pretty base, anyway.

   b. Suppose you find out your partner goes to the horseraces quite regularly in the hope that someday he/she will make a killing at the betting window. What would your reaction be? Check one:
      - ☐ w. Nobody ever wins except the owners. He/She is foolish to bet.
      - ☐ x. People sometimes win, but betting could interfere with his/her regular job. I'd worry.
      - ☐ y. If he/she enjoys it, why not? I might even go along.
      - ☐ z. We will get into debt. I'd try to stop him/her.

   c. Your partner tells you he/she dreams of seeing his/her picture on the cover of *Time* magazine as Man/Woman of the Year. What would your reaction be?
      - ☐ x. Who knows? It *could* happen. It's better to dream than to be satisfied with your present position or achievements.
      - ☐ y. Everyone has a dream like that. It's okay, even if it could never happen.
      - ☐ z. He/She should have his/her feet on the ground, and I'd say so in no uncertain terms.

Please turn the page to find out your score and what it means

SCORING FOR 4

a. If you checked *x*, you're probably being a bit naïve. Score yourself "Average." If you checked *y*, you had a healthy reaction to your partner's fantasy, showing understanding. Score yourself "Excellent." If you checked *z*, you're a bit uptight. Score yourself "Poor." If you checked *w*, you'll need to work on the fantasy problem in your relationship.

b. If you checked *w* or *x*, your attitude is quite normal. You could probably relax a bit about it, though; there are a lot of people who play the horses without becoming hooked on it. Score yourself "Average" in terms of your relationship. If you checked *y*, you've got a good, healthy attitude about the winning fantasy. Score yourself "Good-Excellent." If you checked *z*, your reaction is probably exaggerated. Unless your partner is a pathological gambler, you'll need to work on your own reaction.

c. If you checked *x*, score yourself as "Very good"; you seem to feel your partner's dream moves him/her in the right direction. If you checked *y*, score yourself "Average"; you show some tolerance and understanding for the dream. If you checked *z*, you may need to work on the problem.

Fantasies are often a lot of fun for the person who has them—especially if that person is clear about the difference between fantasy and reality. Trouble arises only when people act as if their fantasies were realities. This kind of trouble can seriously damage any relationship, too, especially if neither partner knows the difference between what they might like to do or be in their wildest dreams and what they can do or be in real life.

By the same token, fantasies are quite normal. Again, if you know the difference between fantasy and reality, fantasies can be great safety valves. If your partner's fantasies seem to be causing trouble in your relationship, the best thing to do is probably to talk about them. It's sometimes hard to get started, but you might learn a great deal about him/her and yourself in the process.

5. *Compliment Department*

Think back to this past week. How many times did you compliment your partner? How many times did he/she compliment you?

Step I

   Circle a number in column A indicating the number of times *you* complimented *your partner* on anything he/she did or said.

Step II

   Circle a number corresponding to the number of times your partner complimented you.

Your Compliments	*Your Partner's Compliments*
A	B
1	1
3	3
5	5
7	7
10	10
12	12
15	15
17	17
20	20
21	21
23	23
over 25	over 25

Please turn the page to find out your score and what it means

SCORING FOR 5

If both partners are equal in their number of compliments, or differ only 1 to 3 points.   *Excellent*

If partners differ by 4 to 6 points.   *Very good*

If they differ by 6 to 9 points.   *Good*

If they differ more than 9 points.   *Poor*

Compliments are more than politeness. They are a sign that you appreciate your partner, that he/she makes a positive difference in your life.

6. *Complaint Department*

Think back to last week. How many times did you complain to or about your partner? How many times do you think your partner complained to or about you?

Step I

Circle a number in column A indicating the number of times you complained to or about your partner.

Step II

Circle a number in column B corresponding to the number of times your partner complained to or about you.

Your Complaints	Your partner's complaints
A	B
1	1
3	3
5	5
7	7
10	10
12	12
15	15
17	17
20	20
21	21
23	23
over 25	over 25

Please turn the page to find out your score and what it means

SCORING FOR 6

If both partners are equal in their number of
complaints, or differ only 1 to 3 points.   *Excellent*

If partners differ by 4 to 6 points.   *Very good*

If they differ by 6 to 9 points.   *Good*

If they differ by more than 9 points.   *Poor*

While a free and understanding relationship should allow
for some general griping, *too much* on the part of one person or
too much generally will eventually destroy any relationship.

7. Affection

Think back over the past week. How many times did you show affection for your partner in some way—a kiss, a special dinner, a thoughtful gesture? How many times did your partner show affection for you?

Step I

Circle a number in column A indicating the number of times you showed affection for your partner.

Step II

Circle a number in column B corresponding to the number of times your partner showed affection for you.

You showed affection	Your partner showed affection
A	B
1	1
3	3
5	5
7	7
10	10
12	12
15	15
17	17
20	20
21	21
23	23
over 25	over 25

Please turn the page to find out your score and what it means

SCORING FOR 7

If both partners are equal in the number of shows
of affection, or differ only 1 to 3 points. *Excellent*

If partners differ by 4 to 6 points. *Very good*

If both partners differ by 6 to 9 points. *Good*

If they differ by more than 9 points. *Poor*

Affection is, of course, essential to any lasting relationship;
an outward display indicates that both parties feel comfortable
and secure. However, some people are inhibited about showing
affection openly—but they may still feel very warm toward each
other.

8. *Growth*

Step I

List below all of the interests that you had *before* you got involved with or married your partner. List only those interests in which you were at least *moderately* involved: for example, if you were interested in art but never went to a museum, do not list art. However, if you were interested in music and did go to concerts, list music.

_____

_____

Step II

Now list the new interests that you have developed *since* you met or married your partner. List real interests only—those in which you are at least *moderately* involved.

_____

_____

Step III

List here interests you have lost since marriage or meeting your partner that you are sincerely sorry to have lost. For instance, if you were interested in movies and have not been able to pursue this interest and you are sincerely sorry, list movies. However, if you were interested in fashion, no longer have time for it, and are not really interested any more, do not list fashion.

_____

_____

Step IV

Now, in the appropriate space below, write the *number* of interests gained since marriage or meeting your partner and the *number* of interests lost.

Number of new interests _____

Number of interests lost _____

Please turn the page to find out your score and what it means

SCORING FOR 8

If new interests minus the interests lost equals:

7 to 8—Very good
4 to 6—Average
1 to 3—Below average
-1 to -2—Poor
-3 or -4—Very poor

TOTAL SCORING

We asked you to measure your relationship with your partner in 8 different, important dimensions. Aside from the individual scores for each part, you should pay special attention to areas in which your scores are better or worse than they are in others.

If, for example, your interests have not grown very much since you have been married or involved for a number of years, you have failed to help each other to grow up and develop. You may well decide to set goals—learning a language together, for instance.

A score of "Very good" or "Excellent" in all 8 categories, particularly if you have been married (or involved) long enough, indicates that you have learned how to make your relationship work. A relationship is a task of continuous development, and if your scores were average, there is no reason you can't both try to improve it.

Anything below average should make you careful. By spotting the problem areas, you can take remedial action.

A comparison of your two tests—yours and your partner's—will give you a fairly reliable way of finding out how your partner feels and where discrepancies exist.

PART THREE

How Do You Like Your Work?

We have tried to help you to become aware of your real self, your emotions, and motivations in the first section of this book.

In the second section, we inventoried how well you get along with other people, how good your interpersonal relationships are.

In this section we are trying to complete your self-awareness by testing a number of your attitudes toward another important aspect of your total personality: work.

Are You in the Right Occupation?

"How much do you think he's earning?" is a common question. You are less likely to hear someone ask, "Do you think he's happy in his job?"

Actually, the person who really likes his job is most likely to receive a fat pay envelope. If someone considers his job dull and dreary, the chances are that he won't advance; low income just adds to his original frustration.

What makes a job "right"? The right job is one that pays off in real and personal satisfaction; one that is absorbing and offers a view of greater opportunities.

Anyone who works—whether running a household or reporting to an office—should take stock now and then. To find out if you have the right job, study the eight situations below and give your honest reactions.

●

1. I'm happiest when I'm up to my ears in work.

   ☐ a. Agree
   ☐ b. Disagree

2. I don't mind hard work, but I prefer working at a leisurely, quiet pace.

   ☐ a. Agree
   ☐ b. Disagree

3. It's very important to me that others—my boss, my co-workers, my customers, my family—value my work and express their appreciation.

   ☐ a. Agree
   ☐ b. Disagree

4. I prefer to plan my own work and goals, rather than to have them laid out for me by others or by circumstances.

☐ a. Agree
☐ b. Disagree

5. I enjoy talking about my work with friends and family.

☐ a. Agree
☐ b. Disagree

6. I am usually very glad—and relieved—when the working day is over.

☐ a. Agree
☐ b. Disagree

7. I look forward to greater challenges and demands in my work, and would even ask for them if they weren't presented to me by my boss or my situation.

☐ a. Agree
☐ b. Disagree

8. I look forward to the time when I won't be working full time; then I'll really be able to enjoy myself and life.

☐ a. Agree
☐ b. Disagree

Please turn the page to find out your score and what it means

SCORING

This test should give you some insight into two areas: what your general attitudes toward work are, and whether the work you're doing now fits those attitudes.

For the first part, score yourself in the following way:

1. a = 2
    b = 1
	2. a = 1
	    b = 2
		3. a = 2
		    b = 1
			4. a = 2
			    b = 1

5. a = 2
    b = 1
	6. a = 1
	    b = 2
		7. a = 2
		    b = 1
			8. a = 1
			    b = 2

Your highest score, indicating a very positive attitude toward work, is 16. Either 14 or 15 still shows a very positive work motivation.

10 to 13 is an average score. If you checked 3a or 5a, you want appreciation by others. 1a and 7a may reveal that you are a "workaholic," a person who has to work to be happy.

8 and 9 are low scores. You may need to change your job. If you checked 8a and 6a, you are happiest if you can devote your time to leisure activities.

Now return to the questions, one at a time. Look at your answer and then ask yourself, "Does the work I do now—whether it's in an office or in the home—provide me with the kind of situation I need, according to my answer?"

For example, if you checked "agree" in 1, ask yourself whether your present work does keep you "up to your ears in work." If it does, you have one indication that you are in the right job for you. If it doesn't, you might think about changing your job, or looking for more responsibility in your present job.

Go through the rest of the questions the same way. The composite picture you come up with will tell you a great deal about whether what you've got now is what you really need or want out of a working situation.

What Is Your Leadership Rating?

Most of us would like to say "excellent." Being a leader seems very desirable. We attribute such qualities to politicians or worry if they don't have them.

Leading, however, is a two-way street. No matter how strong your qualifications may be in your own mind, if people don't want to follow you, you can't legitimately call yourself a leader.

Leadership is composed of many facets. Ability to establish confidence, respect, sometimes love is required. You can also lead people by frightening them; this, however, is not the leadership quality we have in mind.

Many individuals are afraid of assuming a leadership role. Others grow into it although they feel at first that they are not qualified. What about you?

Our test is designed to help you measure yourself by thinking back on real situations in your life and projecting yourself into possible future circumstances where leadership may be required.

●

1. Your instructions have not been followed and everything got messed up. What is the likely reason?

   ☐ a. You did not foresee all the blunders your subordinates could make.
   ☐ b. It seems impossible to get halfway intelligent people to work these days.
   ☒ c. You did not explain the assignment in sufficient detail.

2. You are being asked to organize a group of concerned citizens to improve the neighborhood. How would you react?

   ☐ a. Use an excuse, such as being too busy, to get out of it.
   ☐ b. Ask that someone help you and show you the best way of

doing it, preferably someone who had organized such a group before.

☒ c. Be flattered and accept the assignment, even though you have never done anything like that before.

3. Someone higher up in your organization gives an order. What are you most likely to do?

☐ a. Question the wisdom of the order; possibly suggest a substitute solution.

☐ b. Discuss the pros and cons and finally agree.

☐ c. An order is an order and I carry it through as best I can.

4. You read about the chaotic state of affairs in another country. Finally a strong person takes over and puts everything in a better working order.

☐ a. Is he a dictator? I don't know, and if so, so what?

☐ b. It was necessary to introduce strong measures. The people always have to be led; later on they can participate again in decisions.

☐ c. Had the people been properly informed, they would have taken the right measures themselves.

5. You read the following statement: "He was relentless. He drove himself and others. He did not rest until he had reached a goal." What is your reaction?

☐ a. I am just like him.

☐ b. An unhappy person. I prefer to enjoy myself.

☐ c. If he could relax in between, okay; otherwise I pity him.

6. You read in a person's obituary that he never complimented anyone in his organization. He watched every little detail. His office was like a revolving door. Managers were fired at the slightest pretext. He was feared by everybody, but he created a successful company.

☐ a. That is a very heavy price to pay. Probably nobody really liked him.

☐ b. Sometimes that is the only way to weld a complex company together. The end result is really the important thing.

☐ c. He might have been even more successful had he combined some more pleasant and more human aspects with his toughness.

Please turn the page to find out your score and what it means

SCORING

Add your scores according to the following key:

1. a = 2
    b = 1
    c = 3
	2. a = 1
	    b = 3
	    c = 2
		3. a = 3
		    b = 2
		    c = 1

4. a = 1
    b = 3
    c = 2
	5. a = 3
	    b = 1
	    c = 2
		6. a = 1
		    b = 2
		    c = 3

The best score, indicating strong tendencies to lead and to be successful in almost everything you undertake, whether business, civic duties, or politics, is 18 to 15. A mixture of some leadership tendencies and hesitation about taking on too many leadership tasks could be the basis of a lower score of from 10 to 14. The lowest score is 6 to 9.

Not everybody can be a leader. If you wish to develop abilities in this respect, you would be best advised to rely more on discussions and cooperation from the people you work with, rather than simply telling them what to do and expecting blind obedience.

It is true that the tough leader makes things easier for himself for a while at least, and even for the people who must listen to him. Many people prefer to execute orders rather than to assume responsibilities. This is one of the basic problems of democracy in politics and in business as well as in private life. In the long run the more understanding a boss is, the more successful he is likely to be.

How Well Do You Take Criticism?

No one really likes to be criticized. The important thing, however, is not whether we like it, but whether we can take it and profit from it.

If you can take criticism calmly, you can see yourself as others see you. If you decide that the criticism is fair, you are likely to correct your mistake and make faster progress toward your goal.

If you cannot take criticism, you may be resentful and try to shift the blame away from yourself. You may accuse the other person of stupidity, or you may dismiss him as a jealous fault finder. Ironically, you may defend yourself so passionately that your weaknesses stand out clearly.

The more violently you react to criticism, the surer you can be that the criticism is justified. It's as if someone had bumped a bruised spot on your arm. But, if you can take criticism calmly, you have learned to look at yourself critically.

Can you take criticism? Should you have to? To test yourself, study the six situations below. Then, for each, check the one item that most closely describes your own reaction.

●

1. A woman wearing an unusual, high-fashion hat is walking down the street. People stop and stare, point and whisper. If you were the woman wearing the hat, how would you react?

   ☒ a. This hat really is too far-out; I won't wear it again.
   ☐ b. Those people don't know a beautiful hat when they see one.
   ☐ c. Maybe I should have asked someone to help me select it.

2. In the office next to yours, you overhear your boss yelling at one of your colleagues. What is your reaction?

☐ a. Your colleague is right to take offense.
☒ b. He should defend himself.
☐ c. He should learn to do better next time.

3. You are a carpenter who has been hired to put up some bookshelves. You make some minor changes in your customer's design. When he looks at your work, he insists you do it again, the "right" way, that is, the way he wanted it. What would your reaction be?

☐ a. I won't change the design; it's right this way.
☐ b. I am sorry; I will re-do the part.
☒ c. The design is much better this way, and I'll try to convince him why.

4. Which one of the four statements below best describes your own attitude?

☐ a. By and large I don't think I have any more faults than the average person.
☐ b. I have lots of faults and like to have people tell me so I can improve.
☐ c. The less I know about myself, the better; otherwise I might hate myself.
☒ d. I don't think I have much wrong with me; I really think I'm pretty good.

5. At a party, you committed a faux pas, said something stupid. Someone else points it out. What is your most frequent reaction?

☒ a. I reject the criticism as unfair. There was nothing wrong with what I said.
☐ b. I would have apologized anyway; there was no need to rub it in.
☐ c. Yes, you are right. It just slipped out. I should not have said it.

6. You tell someone about your success, show them your work (paintings, books you have written, etc.). They say nothing. What is your response?

☐ a. You say nothing, but you feel bad.
☑ b. You tell them what others said and how they praised your achievement.
☐ c. You start criticizing and belittling your own work.

Please turn the page to find out your score and what it means

SCORING

Add your scores according to the following key:

1. a = 3	2. a = 1	3. a = 1
b = 1	b = 2	b = 3
c = 2	c = 3	c = 2
4. a = 3	5. a = 1	6. a = 3
b = 4	b = 2	b = 2
c = 1	c = 3	c = 1
d = 2		

If you scored from 7 to 9, you can't take it, probably won't admit it even if you're wrong; 10 to 15 shows that you can take criticism if it doesn't hit your sore spots; 16 to 19 means you profit from fair criticism that fits your standards, but usually aren't too easily swayed.

You should be your own critic first. Set your own standards of conduct and the goals you wish to reach. Then learn to criticize your own performance in view of the standards and goals you have set. Once you can do these things, you are ready to accept or reject an outside criticism.

If it is a fair criticism, and fits your own carefully thought-out standards, take the opportunity to correct and improve yourself. If it is pointless, has no bearing on what you want to be or accomplish, reject it. Don't let yourself be blown about like a straw in the wind.

If it is factual criticism—if you are face to face with an actual failure of your own—watch out. Maybe you are way off the track of your goals, or have not been reasonable in setting them up.

If it is simply "loose talk" from a person who criticizes others freely and frequently, you can safely assume that this person is simply trying to divert attention from his own shortcomings.

If it is an unavoidable "shortcoming"—carrot-red hair and freckles, for example—the best way to combat criticism—and teasing—is to make fun of it. You disarm your critic by beating him to the punch.

How Good Are You in an Emergency?

Our ability to handle a job often depends on how well—or poorly—we handle an emergency. One calm person can save a whole panicky office or factory operation, just as one rattled person can bring chaos. The ability to deal with an emergency is a combination of keeping your cool, being able to act quickly, and seeing alternatives others may not see.

Some people seem perfectly equipped to confront emergencies; others simply conk out. How good are *you* in an emergency?

●

1. There is a blackout. None of the electrical equipment in the office works. What are you most likely to do?

   ☐ a. Sit down, relax, and wait until the lights come on again.
   ☐ b. Start a brainstorming session on how office procedures could be improved or how the next day's work could be speeded up.
   ☐ c. Get an office party going and invite everybody to enjoy themselves.

2. A factory worker has an accident. He can't walk. He should be taken to a hospital. There is no stretcher. What would you do?

   ☐ a. Comfort him until a doctor comes.
   ☐ b. Look for a substitute for a stretcher.
   ☐ c. Carry him on my shoulders or between myself and another worker.

3. Everybody is upset. Everything goes wrong. There is complete bedlam.

   ☐ a. I get panicky too, threaten to quit.

☐ b. I set priorities and do one thing after another and don't bother with the others.

☐ c. I shout, get everybody to calm down and give directions.

4. The key to an important storeroom cannot be found.

☐ a. I try to pry the door open.
☐ b. I call a locksmith.
☐ c. I look for a different way of opening the door.

5. Your car breaks down on a lonely road. What would you do?

☐ a. Wait till another car passes by, even though that may be hours.
☐ b. Walk to the nearest dwelling and ask for help.
☐ c. Use a different method.

6. You need the phone number of a business contact. You don't know the exact name or address. You have lost the slip with his name and number.

☐ a. Call the home office and ask them if they know the name or number.
☐ b. Give up and write a letter to the town where he lives in the hope it will reach him.
☐ c. Use a more ingenious method.

Please turn the page to find out your score and what it means

SCORING

Add your score according to the following key:

1. a = 1 b = 3 c = 2	2. a = 1 b = 3 (if close to our solution*) c = 2
3. a = 1 b = 3 c = 2	4. a = 2 b = 1 c = 3 (if close to our solution*)
5. a = 1 b = 2 c = 3 (if close to our solution*)	6. a = 2 b = 1 c = 3 (if close to our solution*)

Our solutions:
2b Use a trench coat or something similar.
4c Unhinge the door.
5c Siphon gas out of car and make a fire nearby.
6c Call someone with same name in phone book. He may know your contact.

15-18: You can adjust and help yourself in a difficult situation. You are resourceful.

11-14: You solve some emergencies well; others baffle you. Analyze each situation to see how it contributes to your score.

6-10: You are easily confused and prefer others to solve a crisis.

Since we all encounter emergencies, it may be helpful if you develop a sort of training program for yourself. Play difficult situations and ask yourself how you would react. By being prepared, you will have recourse to a previously rehearsed situation.

How Does Your Memory Compare with Others'?

Do you forget a name, place, or crucial fact at exactly the wrong moment? A good memory may make a tremendous difference in your work.

The list below sounds crazy, but it was scientifically planned to test your memory. Study the list on the left side for about 25 seconds. Then, cover the list and in the space on the right side, write down as many objects as you can remember. See next page for scoring and explanation.

●

broom	_____
swan	_____
basin	_____
baby	_____
cobweb	_____
brush	_____
lamp	_____
desk	_____
painting	_____
dog	_____
woman	_____
window	_____
paper	_____
horse	_____
candle	_____
typewriter	_____
book	_____
man	_____
stove	_____
bicycle	_____

Please turn the page to find out your score and what it means

SCORING

To score yourself, count the number of objects you remembered. (The list had 20.)

If you remembered 16-20 objects, you have an excellent memory; 10-15, a good memory; 6-9, average; 5 or below, poor.

Good memory depends on the ability to grasp associations, to group together related facts. For example, basin, baby, woman, broom, and cobweb could be grouped together. They all have something to do with housework. Dog, horse, swan, bicycle are related to outdoors. Lamp, candle, desk, book, typewriter are also associated.

You can develop your memory by trying to connect objects or ideas often completely unrelated. This technique serves as a sort of bridge or chain, where each subject reinforces the next, thus facilitating remembering.

How Quickly Do You Catch On?

Dr. Alexander Fleming wanted to grow a certain type of bacteria. He did not succeed; a certain mold developed and always killed the bacteria. At one point he grasped the relationship and decided that the mold that had the power to destroy the bacteria was much more interesting scientifically than the bacteria itself. Penicillin was discovered. Dr. Fleming had grasped a new relationship; he had "caught on."

We are often handicapped by trying to find a solution by means of customary ways of thinking. By looking for new connections and associations we can achieve a breakthrough. This applies to normal work situations as well as to scientific discovery.

How quickly do you catch on? Try the following test.

●

1. Look at the following list of 10 items. Make 5 pairs of the 10 items, matching two items not on the basis of their physical resemblance, but on the basis of a logical principle. Write down the numbers of each pair in the spaces provided.

   (1) Cigarettes   _____ and _____

   (2) Fire

   (3) Volcano   _____ and _____

   (4) Sausage

   (5) Cow   _____ and _____

   (6) Whale

   (7) Soup   _____ and _____

   (8) Baby bottle

   (9) Hot Dog   _____ and _____

   (10) Cavity

2. You are asked to set up an intelligent cross-reference system, which is better than just the usual alphabetical system. For example, a surgeon's job is comparable to the one of a tailor. You should therefore file *surgeon* also under *tailor*. Try such filing systems on each of the following subjects:

Hot dogs   Soap   Pen

3. You find a treasure chest in a clearing in the woods. It is important to establish how long it has been hidden in this grassy spot. How can you tell how long the chest has been there?

4. You have to remind yourself to take medication regularly every four hours. What is the best way of doing it?

☐ a. Ask someone in your family to remind you.
☐ b. Every time you take the drug, set an alarm for four hours from then.
☐ c. Tie the medication in with some other regular activity, such as breakfast, lunch, coffee break, dinner.

5. You are being asked to match sound tracks of voices with movies of men. What would you be looking for to help pair them correctly?

☐ a. Depth of voices.
☐ b. The way they dress, and how clearly they speak.
☐ c. A special kind of activity.

6. A news announcer describes a scene of rioting in a biased way. In which one of the following statements do you recognize his prejudice?

☐ a. "An unruly mob of disgruntled and furious people demonstrated in the street."
☐ b. "Hundreds of angry people gathered in front of the offices of the opposition party."
☐ c. "They made fists in threatening gestures and shouted insults at the people inside the offices, who, frightened by this outburst, locked themselves in."

Please turn the page to find out your score and what it means

SCORING

1. Correct answers are: 1 and 2, 3 and 10, 5 and 6, 8 and 9, 4 and 7.

   1 and 2 glow and burn; 3 and 10 are earth and dental cavities; 5 and 6 are mammals; 8 and 9 are orally satisfying; 4 and 7 are food. Give yourself a score of 1 for each correct pair.

2. *Hot dogs* could be filed with oral pleasures, *soap* with ritual bath and other rituals, *pen* with other instruments for making markings, such as straight pins. Give yourself a 2 for each correct and intelligent filing system.

3. The grass under the chest stopped growing when the chest was hidden in the woods. Near and around the chest, the grass kept growing. By measuring the height of the grass around the chest, and establishing the average growth rate for grass around this time of year, you could calculate how long the chest has been hidden there. (Give yourself a score of 3 for a solution that approximates this one.)

4. a = 1   5. a = 2   6. a = 3
   b = 2   b = 1   b = 2
   c = 3   c = 3 (Smoking a pipe and puffing on the   c = 2
               sound track, or holding hand over
               mouth while coughing, etc.)

Your best total score could be 23. Even a score of 21 is still a sign of easily catching on and being alert.

9-14 would be an indication of a difficulty in grasping somewhat hidden meanings.

15-21, depending on the composition of the score, is a good average. If you do better in the more practical tests (4, 5, or 6), you are quick when pragmatic tasks confront you. The other tests require more abstract thinking, but also independence of approach.

One can learn through examples to recognize pitfalls and acquire a grasp of more complex relations. The ability to catch on is an important quality for scientific work but it is also helpful in many other areas.

How Conscientious Are You?

If you have ever fought a battle with yourself about getting up early to do a necessary job, you have heard two small voices within yourself. One has told you the job is important and must be done. The other has rationalized that it's better to relax until the spirit moves you, that no one will ever know whether you do or don't do the job that day.

That first voice is your conscience. The harder it has to push you to do a necessary job, the less conscientious you are.

During your childhood, your response to the call of duty was first established. It had to do with hanging up your clothes and doing your homework. Sometimes you did the expected thing under your own steam; sometimes it took outside force.

If your childhood training was successful, your conscience has by now developed to a point where it functions without too much strain. You have high standards and you stick to them without outside pressure.

You simply feel that doing your duty is more satisfying than evading it. You are not negligent; you are not a late-comer, postponer, or goldbricker.

What are *your* standards? There is a happy medium between the stickler for details and the negligent person with few standards. To test yourself, study the situations below. Then, for each, check the caption that describes your reaction.

●

1. A girl is lying on her bed, hands behind her head, in the midst of a very messy room. Clothes, books, and papers are strewn all around.

    ☐ a. She will straighten up the room before she goes to bed tonight.

    ☐ b. She just doesn't care about the disorder; she's working on an idea.

    ☐ c. She'll clean it up in the morning; she's busy at other things now.

2. A group of men are sitting around a conference table. The man at the head of the table is pounding his fist on the table.

☐ a. The president has been asked to reconsider his viewpoint. He refuses.

☐ b. He may compromise if they will meet him halfway; they have a point.

☐ c. He is going to give in; he doesn't want to make any enemies.

3. A group of young people are sitting around a picnic table, obviously enjoying themselves.

☐ a. Serious problems don't hold any interest for them. Why should they?

☐ b. They're young, have no worries. It's all right if they're in the mood.

☐ c. They seem irresponsible, interested only in themselves and their fun.

4. Check the letter next to the person with whom you'd most enjoy prolonged companionship.

☐ a. A happy housewife: fresh, wholesome, and natural.

☐ b. A well-dressed woman, checking a schedule: bright, chic young executive.

☐ c. An artist painting a landscape: artistic, creative, individual.

5. You did not finish the work you promised yourself you would get done. A friend comes to visit and tells you to do it tomorrow. What is your reaction?

☐ a. He is right; no sense knocking myself out.

☐ b. I am too tired anyway. Tomorrow I will be fresh and will be done in no time.

☐ c. I just won't be able to sleep or relax. I had better finish it now.

6. You discover that one of your colleagues left out certain sections of a report, apparently because he thought that would save time and no one would notice it. Your reaction, please?

☐ a. I will make the necessary corrections or fill in the missing part myself.

☐ b. I will call the negligent person to task and force him to re-do what has been left out.

☐ c. It would probably not make any difference anyway. I will let it go.

Please turn the page to find out your score and what it means

SCORING

Add your score according to the following key:

1.	a = 3		2.	a = 3		3.	a = 1
	b = 1			b = 2			b = 2
	c = 2			c = 1			c = 3

4.	a = 2		5.	a = 1		6.	a = 3
	b = 3			b = 2			b = 2
	c = 1			c = 3			c = 1

6-9: you are not very conscientious, you try to avoid responsibility.

10-12 shows a fair balance of conscientiousness.

13-15 means that you are well equipped to do conscientious work, sometimes are even too demanding of yourself and others.

16-18 shows that you are overconscientious; it would be good to look into your standards, accept the fact that different ways of living are as right for other people as yours are for you.

To a certain extent, our standards are established by the group within which we live. A person with even a low degree of conscientiousness can muddle along successfully in a negligent group. But a person living or working with perfectionists has to watch his step all the time.

If you set your standards too high, and are overconscientious about trying to fulfill them, you are indulging in a form of self-protection. You want to be perfect, so that no one can find fault with you. You are afraid of the slightest criticism.

On the other hand, you may be underconscientious, careless about tasks assigned to you. The explanation is that you rely on others. You put your load on their shoulders.

Do You Work Better Alone or in a Group?

Some of us are loners in a working situation. We have difficulty assigning and delegating jobs to others. Sometimes we are convinced that we can do most things better than others; sometimes we feel uncomfortable about having to share success or failure with other people. Knowing whether you work better alone or in a group can make a big difference in choosing the right occupation or role within an organization.

Many tasks are actually best performed by people who prefer to work by themselves; others cannot be accomplished unless a group effort is involved. The astronauts' landing on the moon, for example, involved literally hundreds of people. The artist or writer, on the other hand, does things more comfortably by himself or herself.

Find out in which situation you feel most comfortable. This awareness may guide you in either changing your present work arrangement or, if you have no other choice, to learn to work alone or to try to get along with others.

•

1. You see a sign on the wall of a colleague's office saying: "I do it myself." What is your reaction?

   ☒ a. I feel the same way. He is my kind of person.
   ☐ b. He is arrogant. I'd like to know just how many things he really can accomplish all by himself.
   ☐ c. He does not quite mean what the sign says. He is a proud guy but I am sure he accepts and likes help.

2. You have been part of a complex and very successful building project or scientific task. What makes you feel most proud?

   ☐ a. My ideas were on the right track. I worked most of the solutions out myself.

☐ b. I learned a lot from my colleagues, and made many friends.

☑ c. We all solved the problem jointly. A wonderful team.

3. If you were a musician, what would you see yourself as?

☐ a. Conductor.

☐ b. Member of a trio or quartet.

☑ c. Member of a great orchestra.

4. You are admiring the Pyramids or a great work of architecture. What are you most likely thinking about while looking at the object?

☐ a. What a great architect and engineer designed this project.

☐ b. He must have known how to organize the work and got the cooperation of his co-workers.

☑ c. Imagine how many people must have labored on this job to get it accomplished.

5. You are given an assignment either to paint a house, to develop a fashion department, or to set up a schedule for efficient operation of a factory. What would be your first move?

☐ a. Lock yourself up in an office or workroom and think the whole project through; then assign the tasks.

☑ b. Call possible collaborators together and ask them to contribute their ideas and meet with you afterward.

☐ c. Organize the job in various specialties and skills and make one person responsible for each particular area.

6. You read about a company that failed soon after the president died or got ill.

☐ a. It was to be expected. He never could build an organization.

☐ b. It would have happened regardless. That is the kind of business or operation it was.

☐ c. Had he delegated authority, someone like me could have helped and several of us could have built a viable organization that would have survived.

Please turn the page to find out your score and what it means

SCORING

Add your scores according to the following key:

1. a = 3
   b = 1
   c = 2
	2. a = 3
	   b = 2
	   c = 1
		3. a = 3
		   b = 2
		   c = 1

4. a = 3
   b = 2
   c = 1
	5. a = 3
	   b = 2
	   c = 1
		6. a = 2
		   b = 3
		   c = 1

The highest score, showing the greatest ability or preference to work alone, is between 15 and 18. You are at your best when all the responsibility is yours.

A score of 10 to 14—depending of course on how it is composed—points out your desire to organize things but also your ability to cooperate and work with a group.

6-9 makes you a good person within a group. You like to be with co-workers and feel more comfortable in such situations.

Why is it harder to say "We did it" than "I did it?" Partnerships frequently split up because people cannot work together. One partner or another may feel that sharing the credit for a job means a personal loss for him or her.

If you work with another person on a job, the two of you usually produce a better result, or at least a satisfactory one, in half the time. The credit due is then twice what it would have been for one person working alone, and is enough for both.

Most of us feel that working together pays, or we wouldn't get married, form associations, start partnerships. But we need to learn more about cooperating with others. Even a concert soloist must depend on the cooperation of others: the audience, music critics, press agents, stagehands.

You can "compete as a cooperator" by fitting your special talents in with those of others; successful managers do this. And you can arrange cooperative projects in such a way that each person realizes the benefits to him. The greatest benefits—including personal prestige and achievement—generally come from working closely with others.

How Efficient Are You?

Many work difficulties arise because people are not properly prepared or have not thought ahead. They start a job and discover they need more material or don't have the proper tools. Others make a careful list and consider all alternatives.

While some people seem able to build, work, write in an intuitive fashion, developing ideas and procedures as they go along, most people seem to produce better results by thinking things through ahead of time and figuring out what the proper step-by-step procedure ought to be. We call these people *efficient*. They seem to be able to get things done on time, to avoid too many mistakes or at least learn from the mistakes they do make.

How efficient are you? Take the following quiz to help find out:

●

1. Do you keep a date book?

    ☐ a. Yes, on a day-by-day basis.
    ☐ b. On and off. I start one and then I neglect it.
    ☐ c. I think it is a waste of time. Things have a way of changing too much, anyway.

2. How do you use a calendar?

    ☐ a. Only to look at today's date.
    ☐ b. I mark down a few birthdays.
    ☐ c. My calendar is kept up-to-date and is filled with plans for almost the whole year ahead.

3. When you are about to visit a friend and don't have exact instructions on how to get there, what do you usually do?

    ☐ a. I ask for exact instructions and mark them on a road map.

    ☐ b. I just drive more or less in the direction where I remember they live and I often get lost.

    ☐ c. I stop on the way a few times and ask for directions.

4. When you plan to have things done for a particular day or week . . .

    ☐ a. I usually get things done the way I planned them.
    ☐ b. It hardly ever works out the way I planned it; something always goes wrong.
    ☐ c. I plan in such a way that there is leeway for some changes.

5. You have the following tasks to accomplish. Arrange them in the order by which you get them all done in the least amount of time.

    ☐ a. Pick up a parcel. It is heavy. The place closes at 11 A.M.
    ☐ b. Buy frozen food.
    ☐ c. You have no cash. You need money. Go to bank.
    ☐ d. Your car is almost out of gas. Go to gas station.
    ☐ e. Have lawnmower repaired. He promised to have it ready in an hour if you dropped it off in time.
    ☐ f. Pick up a friend at the railroad station. Train arrives at 12 noon.
    ☐ g. Pick up repaired lawnmower.

6. Which of the following items do you have at home right now?

    ☐ Candles or flashlight in case of a blackout.
    ☐ A list of all valuables that could be stolen, with their serial numbers.
    ☐ Extra keys in separate places.
    ☐ The numbers of your credit cards.
    ☐ A list of where your will and other important documents are.
    ☐ A battery-operated radio.
    ☐ A folder with instructions on how to get to your friends' homes.
    ☐ A time schedule of commuter trains, if you live in the suburbs, or a public transportation map, if you live in the city.

Please turn the page to find out your score and what it means

SCORING

Add your score according to the following key:

1. a = 3	2. a = 1	3. a = 3	4. a = 3
b = 2	b = 2	b = 1	b = 1
c = 1	c = 3	c = 2	c = 2

5. Give yourself the following scores, according to how you arranged the sequence:

Score 4	Score 3	Score 1
c	c	a
d	e	b
e	d	c
a	b	d
f	g	e
g	a	f
b	f	g

(There is no score of 2, since we jump from a reasonable sequence to an inefficient one.)

6. Give yourself 1 point for each item.

Your best score: 24. You are very efficient. It should show up in your work and in the way you tackle most jobs.

A score of 20 to 23 is also an indication of efficiency, although not in all areas.

The lowest score is 8 to 14. You lack foresight. You prefer to do things more intuitively. Of course, many people get things accomplished that way, too, but some effort and planning may save you time and energy.

15-19, depending on how your score is arrived at, puts you into the broad category of most of us. Sometimes you muddle through, but you make enough attempts to organize your work and activities to pass as a halfway efficient person.

You can train yourself to be more efficient, particularly if you begin to realize how much better you can use the time saved for leisure activities and fun.

How Good Are You at Making Decisions?

We have to make decisions almost continually about jobs, political candidates, friends, how to arrange our life styles. Yet few of us have ever taken the time to learn how to make decisions.

This test is designed to acquaint you with your own qualities as a decision maker. Approach each series of choices with an open mind and observe *how* you go about making up your mind. For this exercise to be effective, it is important for you to project yourself into each suggested situation as if it were really happening in your life.

●

1. You have to make a choice among three new fashion models. Which would you pick?

   ☐ a. Very chic, ultra-modern dress.
   ☐ b. Modern, but not obviously out to impress.
   ☐ c. Conservative, quietly elegant.

2. You need a good assistant for your journalistic work. Which type would you hire?

   ☐ a. Bright, quick, but unsystematic.
   ☐ b. Competitive, creative, interested in moving ahead.
   ☐ c. Very reliable, carries tasks through on his/her own, but seldom generates original ideas.

3. How would you decorate your office?

   ☐ a. Unusual design, colors, and furniture.
   ☐ b. To complement your own personality: if you are small then small patterns, intimate; if you are exuberant, then big designs, etc.
   ☐ c. Functional, modern, good taste, but no showing-off.

4. You have just met three new women/men. With which one would you go out first?

    ☐ a. Warm, somewhat shy and timid, needs mothering, protecting.

    ☐ b. Accepting women and men as equal, not too tied up with traditional roles.

    ☐ c. Strong, self-assured, successful.

5. You have been offered three new jobs. Which one would you take?

    ☐ a. One offering freedom, not much security, but great challenge.

    ☐ b. Steady, secure, quite interesting.

    ☐ c. Hectic, creative, having to work with a great teacher.

6. You earn an extra $4,000 as a bonus. What would you spend your money on?

    ☐ a. New car.

    ☐ b. Unusual vacation.

    ☐ c. Fancy new apartment.

Please turn the page to find out your score and what it means

SCORING

In order to help you find out what kind of decision maker you really are, we tricked you a little bit. We are not as interested in the specific decisions you made as in *how* you made your decisions.

Go back to each of your choices and fill in the following information about each on Chart 1 below. Remember, treat each decision as if it were a *real* one.

1. In the first column put down how long you estimate it took you to make up your mind—in minutes or seconds.
2. In the second column check whether you weighed the pros and cons or not.
3. In the third column check the mood—very relaxed to very tense—you were in after you made your decision.
4. In the fourth column put down next to each choice how definite you feel about it—were you certain or did you still have doubts?
5. In the last column put down your reaction to being told that you should have chosen an alternative different from the one you actually chose. Would you be angry, defensive, ready to stick to your decision, or be willing to reconsider?

Add all the scores in each column and divide by 6. The result is your average for each column.

On the decision-making profile chart (Chart 2 below), mark the average score for each column with a dot or cross on the vertical line.

Connect the dots. The graph that results will give you an interesting decision-making profile of yourself.

There are no "good" or "bad" answers. If you are careful when you make decisions, check the pros and cons, and do not regret your decisions, you might fare better in general, particularly if you can defend your decision.

If you take a long time to make a decision, but then decide impulsively simply because you cannot or did not want to weigh the alternatives calmly, and if you have doubts afterward, training in more deliberate decision making may help you to avoid mistakes.

CHART 1

DECISION	TIME	HOW MADE?	HOW DID YOU FEEL ABOUT IT?	ARE YOU SURE?	IS YOUR MIND MADE UP?
	Actual time to make decision (min. or sec.)	Very impulsive 1 Somewhat impulsive 2 In between 3 Somewhat deliberate 4 Very deliberate 5 *Score*	Very relaxed 1 Somewhat relaxed 2 Balanced 3 Somewhat tense 4 Very tense 5 *Score*	Very definite 1 Somewhat definite 2 In between 3 Somewhat indefinite 4 Very indefinite 5 *Score*	Will reconsider 1 May reconsider 2 Casual consideration 3 Probably stick to decision 4 Definitely stick to decision 5 *Score*
1					
2					
3					
4					
5					
6					

CHART 2

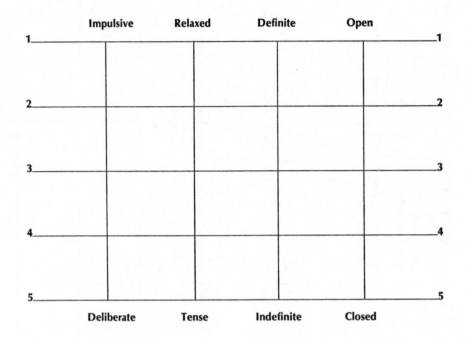

Would You Make a Good Boss?

Being on my own. Not having to take orders, not being at somebody else's beck and call. Haven't we all dreamed about that?

If you are a boss, this test will make you aware of some of the strengths or shortcomings of your "boss role." You can then take appropriate action to correct or further improve some of these attitudes.

If you have been considering becoming your own boss, you may want to know to what extent you have the proper qualifications. You may feel that if you have them, you should go ahead; if you don't, you may either want to develop the necessary qualities or continue to work for someone else.

The following test may give you some help in developing your profile as a boss—or a potential boss.

●

1. You discover that a subordinate has developed a new idea that is better than yours. What would you do?

   ☐ a. Be somewhat annoyed, but encourage him and congratulate him.
   ☐ b. Try to find fault with the idea.
   ☐ c. Feel happy that you have found such a good pupil.

2. A report from one of your associates turns out to be a disappointing piece of work. Would you . . .

   ☐ a. try to find new and interesting "twists" to give it more value?
   ☐ b. throw up your hands in dismay?
   ☐ c. ask your associate to do it over and accept the delay?

3. At an office party, a colleague who is somewhat tipsy suddenly says to you, "You are a real jerk." What would you do?

- [ ] a. Answer him similarly.
- [ ] b. Laugh, but be secretly annoyed.
- [ ] c. Resolve to talk to him about it when he is sober again.

4. You come across a magazine feature on marketing for the 1980s. What would your attitude be?

- [ ] a. Interesting but of no value.
- [ ] b. Crystal-ball nonsense.
- [ ] c. Might have important implications for my business.

5. You have given an order. In spite of its urgency, your instructions were not followed. What would you do?

- [ ] a. Confront the guilty party angrily.
- [ ] b. Shrug and do it yourself.
- [ ] c. Discuss with your colleagues how such a delay may be avoided in the future.

6. You read about a company that has made a fortune because it had the foresight to enter a risky venture. What would your attitude be?

- [ ] a. They were just lucky.
- [ ] b. That's the only avenue open to modern companies.
- [ ] c. Even if they had lost out, it could have been a valuable experience.

7. You have to cut down on staff because of recession or slowdown of business. Which alternatives would you choose?

- [ ] a. Fire the poorest performers at your discretion.
- [ ] b. Ask the staff to make suggestions on how to cut down (fewer working hours for everybody, for example).
- [ ] c. Fire the ones suggested by staff.

8. Your sales have been declining steadily over the past few months. What would you do?

   ☐ a. Cut down on overhead immediately.
   ☐ b. Invest in new promotion ideas.
   ☐ c. Wait it out.

9. Somebody has done a good job. What do you usually do or think you would do?

   ☐ a. Praise him or her for a job well done.
   ☐ b. Praise, but mix it with some points on how it could have been done better.
   ☐ c. Praise him or her, but explain why it has been a good job and why you are satisfied.

10. You have an opportunity to become a partner in a new company. Which financial arrangement would you prefer?

   ☐ a. High guaranteed salary.
   ☐ b. Lower guaranteed salary plus profit sharing.
   ☐ c. Lower guaranteed salary plus stock options.

11. You are in a bad mood, for personal or business reasons. What would you do?

   ☐ a. Blow your top at your staff without realizing why or realizing only when it is too late.
   ☐ b. Refuse to see anyone until you have cooled off.
   ☐ c. Blow your top and then apologize.

12. You have been invited to participate in a panel discussion of problems facing your industry in the next decade. What would your approach be?

   ☐ a. The industry should investigate the roots of the problems.
   ☐ b. Your industry has always faced problems.
   ☐ c. There are uncontrollable factors contributing to the industry's problems.

Please turn the page to find out your score and what it means

SCORING

Score your answers for each question. (Notice carefully the number of each question; they are *not* in order.):

A	B	C	D
1. a = 2 b = 1 c = 3	2. a = 3 b = 1 c = 2	3. a = 3 b = 2 c = 1	4. a = 2 b = 1 c = 3
7. a = 1 b = 3 c = 2	8. a = 1 b = 3 c = 2	5. a = 3 b = 2 c = 1	6. a = 1 b = 3 c = 2
9. a = 2 b = 1 c = 3	12. a = 3 b = 2 c = 1	11. a = 3 b = 1 c = 2	10. a = 1 b = 3 c = 2

We grouped these questions the way we did because each column indicates different qualities of a boss: democratic, optimistic, emotional, and foresighted. All four qualities are important in modern management.

Column A. Are you democratic?
Column B. Are you optimistic?
Column C. Do you control your emotions?
Column D. Do you have foresight?

At the bottom of each column above, add up the total score. Now look at the interpretations below for a profile of you as a boss:

In each category, your score could range from 3 to 9. You can develop a profile for yourself by finding out in which one of the categories you score highest. If your score was 9 in the "democratic" group, you tend to be democratic.

A score of 9 and 8 in the emotional group means that you are very emotional. A score of 3 and 4 in this category shows that you are a cool person: usually this is more desirable in a boss. You might be, as many of us are, a mixture between cool and warm; your score would then be 5, 6, or 7.

Optimism is another essential quality in conducting a business as an entrepreneur or a boss. A score of 9 and 8 shows that you can weather many difficulties and see the brighter side of things.

Foresight is equally important. Every business has its ups and downs. Knowing ahead of time, by proper planning, what might happen, and preparing things accordingly, will make you a better manager. A score of 8 or 9 indicates you anticipate developments.

All four qualities are essential; they are the psychological faculties you need in addition to the technical knowledge your specific job or occupation requires.

Are You Really Ambitious?

Some people reach the peak of their ambitions at twenty, others are still trying to move ahead at eighty. What about you? Are you expecting too much of yourself, or too little?

Imagine yourself as you hope to be five years from now, when some of your present plans and dreams have been realized. Do you expect to have a larger home, a better job, more interesting friends? All of us set future goals for ourselves. Some of us set these goals very high, and "hitch our wagons to a star." Others of us demand less of life and of ourselves.

Take stock of yourself: Consider your abilities and your present position. How much can you reasonably expect to improve your life within the next five years? Have you set yourself a goal that is far beyond your present achievement, or are you nearly satisfied with your life as it is now?

●

1. At a staff meeting, your boss indicates he is concerned about a particular problem in the company. Most of all, he's concerned about the apparently total lack of information about the situation. Which of the following reactions do you identify with?

   ☐ a. I could offer to study the problem and write up a short report for the boss.
   ☐ b. I would suggest that a study be made, but I couldn't possibly manage it myself.
   ☐ c. I'd worry that the boss would ask me to help gather information about the problem, and would try to avoid having to do it.

2. At a community meeting, you see a notice posted asking for volunteers to organize a citizens' group for the purpose of getting the mayor's office to act on a traffic safety program that has been

sitting on his desk for several months. Which of the following would be your most probable reaction?

☐ a. I've been looking for some way to get involved in community affairs. This may be just the ticket.

☐ b. It certainly is a worthy cause. Maybe I'd join up if I could get a couple of my friends to get involved, too.

☐ c. I hope they get somebody to do that. It's high time the problem got solved.

3. You read a story about a twenty-eight-year-old woman who has just become a member of the New York Stock Exchange. According to the story, she plans to expand her business soon. Which of the following comes closest to your reaction?

☐ a. I wish I could do that, but I just don't think I have what it takes to make it big.

☐ b. Does she think she has to prove something? She must, she's so aggressive. How else could she have made it in that world?

☐ c. I'd really like to spend a couple of hours talking with her. Maybe I'd learn something about how she got to where she is.

4. You are going on a business trip to Mexico within two months. You don't speak Spanish. What will you do?

☐ a. Take an intensive course.

☐ b. Most people I'll meet will speak English anyway.

☐ c. I'll learn just enough Spanish to order a meal and ask for directions.

5. You have a chance to make extra money by working during your vacation. You have a good income, but the extra money would be welcome.

☐ a. I'll insist on my vacation and forgo the extra income.

☐ b. I'll cut my vacation and make use of this opportunity.

☐ c. I'll try to do both: cut my vacation short but not forgo it completely, and make some, but not all, of the extra money.

6. You have a good job with security. Every year or so you can count on a raise. You are suddenly being offered a big opportunity in another city with a different unknown company. What will be your decision?

- ☐ a. Accept, after some investigation. One has to look out for oneself.
- ☐ b. Reject such uncertainty. I am well-off where I am. I don't want to conquer the world.
- ☐ c. I will take a sabbatical for a month and try the new job.

Please turn the page to find out your score and what it means

SCORING

1. a = 3	2. a = 3	3. a = 2
b = 2	b = 2	b = 1
c = 1	c = 1	c = 3
4. a = 3	5. a = 1	6. a = 3
b = 1	b = 3	b = 1
c = 2	c = 2	c = 2

If your score is 16 to 18, depending on your values, ambition can be good or bad. You are always seeing goals ahead of you rather than being satisfied with what you are.

If you score 11 to 15, your drive is moderate. Much depends of course on the area of your ambition. You may be interested in community and political recognition, which is different from wanting to get ahead in your occupation or learning a new language.

A score of 6 to 10 is fairly low. Psychologically, you have to differentiate between a real lack of ambition and the fear of tackling new tasks and testing your ability. Many times the real explanation of a low ambition rating is the lack of belief in yourself.

Whether people who are satisfied with a more quiet and not particularly aggressive life style are happier than those who are continuously striving is now being questioned more frequently than it was one or two decades ago.

Is Being Logical Important to You?

What is logic? The classic example is proper deduction: if A is bigger than B and C is bigger than A, which one—A, B, or C—is the largest? The answer is, of course C.

We also need logical thinking in our everyday life. Many right or wrong decisions are based on logical or illogical thinking. In planning something like a trip, you obviously will not start out with the furthest place, then backtrack, unless you have a good reason for doing so, which has nothing to do with logic.

Good mathematicians use logic; so do musicians. A good mechanic is usually someone who can figure out by a process of elimination what could possibly have gone wrong; he eliminates one source of trouble after another in a *logical* way until he has discovered the trouble spot.

Find out how logical you are in various circumstances. What are the logical solutions to this quiz?

●

1. Clarify this sentence (use the space below):

   "We are asking that by the committee report and other expressions of legislative intent the committee clearly indicate that it is not the intention of the legislation to impede the development and utilization of devices which are essentially psychological rather than medical in nature."

   _____

   _____

   _____

2. Order these sentences correctly:
   (a) Man falls down the stairs.
   (b) Ambulance in front of private house.
   (c) Family visits man in hospital.
   (d) Man climbs ladder in file room.
   (e) Ambulance in front of office building.
   (f) Man walking with cane on sidewalk.

   _____

3. What is wrong with this set of instructions? (Jot down your answer in the space below.)

   "Unwrap the toaster. Fasten the handles with the plastic paste provided, to both sides of the toaster. Insert the grill with the baking side up and you are ready for the most delicious English muffins."

   _____

   _____

4. For each word below, think of three other words with similar meanings.

   Opening: _____, _____, _____

   Event: _____, _____, _____

   Guarantee: _____, _____, _____

   Renew: _____, _____, _____

5. A single two-story five-year-old building collapses. What is the most logical explanation?

   ☐ a. An earthquake
   ☐ b. Weak construction
   ☐ c. Shift in ground under foundation.

Please turn the page to find out your score and what it means

SCORING

1. The best answer would be something like:
   "The committee should clarify the legal distinction between medical and psychological devices."
   Rate your answer from 3 (very close) to 1 (very different).

2. d, e, c, f, a, b
   The correct answer depends on your discovery that the man had a second accident: falling down the stairs. If your order was the same as ours, you score 3; if not, 0.

3. There are three mistakes:
   (1) Plastic paste would melt.
   (2) Which is the baking side? It was not explained.
   (3) The instructions failed to mention to plug the toaster in.
   Give yourself 1 point for each mistake you found in the instructions; 0 if you found none.

4. Opening: window, hole, door
   Event: happening, occurrence, incident
   Guarantee: vouch, safeguard, warranty
   Renew: recondition, renovate, re-do
   Give yourself 1 point for each good set. (It does not have to be the same as ours.)

5. a = 1   b = 2   c = 3

   Your best score would be 16. Even a score of 15 or 14 shows that you can think logically in various areas, verbal as well as practical.

   A score of 7 to 13 puts you among most of us. If the composition of your score results from tests 1 and 4, you are more gifted in verbal logic. 2, 3, and 5 test more three-dimensional and practical logic.

   A low score is 3 to 6. You might benefit by practicing on some other logical problems. Try to recognize cause and effect relationships and figuring out associations between things, ideas, and situations.

What Kind of Work Do You Really Like?

A brief test, by itself, won't tell you precisely what kind of occupation you're best suited for. The test that follows will, we hope, help you analyze some of the motivations you have in work situations and some of the satisfactions you seek.

Some people need visual satisfactions; they want to *see* what they are working on. Others aim for more tactile achievements; they want to *feel* it. Others, again, want to work with abstract ideas.

Often we are mistaken about our own preferences. We may wind up expressing our desires in hobbies instead of our regular jobs.

The following questions deal with various elements of a work situation. Read the phrase at the beginning of each question, then respond to the question that accompanies it.

●

1. *You and your colleagues.* Which of these descriptions best represents your feelings on *how you want to relate* to other people in your job?

   ☐ a. I am a leader among my co-workers.
   ☐ b. I am told what to do by others.
   ☐ c. Some of my colleagues are on the same level; others are below me.

2. *Materials.* I *prefer* to work with . . .

   ☐ a. wood, steel, stone.
   ☐ b. textiles, plastic.
   ☐ c. paint, tile.
   ☐ d. paper, books.
   ☐ e. people (children, mature, older).

3. *Rewards.* Pick one type of reward you would *prefer:*

☐ a. Normal pay, no risks.
☐ b. Good pay, some risks.
☐ c. Excellent pay, lots of risks.

4. *Relation to company.* What kind of relationship do you *prefer* with a company or group?

☐ a. You are a cog in the machine.
☐ b. You are an integral part of the operation.
☐ c. You are a big wheel in the company.

5. *Sociability.* How do you *prefer* to relate to individuals in a job?

☐ a. I prefer to be alone.
☐ b. I like the companionship of one person.
☐ c. I enjoy a small group.
☐ d. Large groups are best for me.

6. *Results.* I *prefer* work where the results of my efforts are . . .

☐ a. immediately visible.
☐ b. visible within a short time.
☐ c. visible in one month.
☐ d. visible in three months.
☐ e. visible in one year.
☐ f. never visible to me.

7. *Tempo and rhythm.* What tempo, or pace of work, *is most pleasing* to you?

☐ a. An even, step-wise progression.
☐ b. Secure and protected, quiet.
☐ c. Ups and downs, lots of excitement.
☐ d. A melodious rhythm.

8. *Body.* Which parts of your body *would you want* to be employed most of the time in your work?

☐ a. Eyes.
☐ b. Brain.
☐ c. Hands.
☐ d. Legs.
☐ e. Arms.
☐ f. Total body.

Please turn the page to find out your score and what it means

SCORING

On the top of the master chart that follows, you will find the numbers of the questions in the quiz. Under each appear the letters corresponding to the answers for each question. Circle the letter on the chart that corresponds to the letter you checked when you took the quiz. Now go down the column under that letter and circle all the x's in that column. (For example, if your answer for 1 was *a,* you will have circled all the x's—there are 10—under the *a* column for 1.)

Follow the same procedure for each numbered question. When you have completed this process, look at the *horizontal* rows and find the one in which you have most x's circled. To the left of this row, you will find the name of the occupation you might very well be most happy in, based on your answers to the quiz. The row that contains the next-highest number of circled x's may point you in the direction of an alternative occupation—or a hobby.

You can also use this chart to find out the difference between what you *are* doing and what you would *want* to do by filling out the chart twice, once for your present occupation and a second time for your dream.

Many of us, even after we have been in a field for many years, may be tempted to give ourselves a second chance. This test might show up some of these hidden desires and dreams. Good luck!

	1. Your Colleagues				2. Materials					3. Rewards			4. Relation to company			5. Sociability				6. Results						7. Tempo				8. Body					
	a	b	c	d	a	b	c	d	e	a	b	c	a	b	c	a	b	c	d	a	b	c	d	e	f	a	b	c	d	a	b	c	d	e	f
Architect			X	X	X							X	X		X	X						X		X				X		X	X				
Interior decorator			X			X			X		X		X		X	X	X					X		X				X		X	X	X			
Sculptor					X										X	X							X				X			X		X			
Painter							X					X			X	X							X	X			X					X			
Entrepreneur									X			X	X		X	X				X				X											
Fashion designer		X				X			X	X		X					X				X		X				X			X	X				
Furniture designer		X						X	X	X		X					X				X		X				X			X	X	X			
Layout artist				X				X	X	X							X			X			X							X					
Sales	X											X				X					X							X			X				
Promotion				X					X								X	X			X	X					X			X		X			
Nurse				X				X									X	X			X	X				X						X	X		
Child Care								X					X				X	X		X						X									
Teacher	X											X	X		X		X				X							X		X	X				
Physician	X												X		X						X							X							
Secretary			X					X	X		X			X		X	X			X		X				X				X	X	X			
Librarian									X		X		X			X	X			X		X					X	X		X	X				
Writer									X		X			X		X	X			X							X		X	X	X				
Manager	X							X	X		X				X	X					X		X				X			X	X				
Buyer	X								X		X				X	X					X		X			X	X			X	X				
Administrator	X								X		X		X			X					X		X							X					
Research	X												X		X	X	X					X						X		X	X				
Scientist			X						X		X				X	X					X			X		X				X	X				
Copywriter		X									X				X	X		X							X	X		X		X	X				
Journalist										X	X				X			X		X											X				
Performer	X												X		X	X				X							X		X						X
Singer	X											X			X	X				X							X		X						X
Model			X		X						X						X			X						X									X

A Last Word

The human personality consists of many facets, most of them not clearly separable. Even though we attempted in this book to help you to establish an inventory—an awareness of yourself—the titles of the quizzes we have used are by necessity artificial separations of the complex system we as human beings consist of.

It would have been wonderful to be able to present you with various moving models of motivational engines, and to ask you to select the one that came closest to providing an understanding of your nature. So far, however, that kind of tool for self-knowledge is just a dream.

Despite all this, we hope that by helping you evaluate (honestly, we hope) the three major aspects of how you function—the way you feel about yourself, the way you relate and interact with other people, and how you feel about work—we have provided you with a new way of looking at yourself.

Now that you've gone through the quizzes yourself, you may want to have your partners or your friends fill out the same quizzes *about you*. Comparing your self-appraisal with the judgment of your friends and co-workers could be very revealing and useful, though it may also be uncomfortable at times.

Whether you accept this increased awareness of yourself as simply an interesting psychological X-ray, or whether you decide to change certain behavior and attitudes as a result of that awareness, is up to you. In the end, the important question to ask yourself is whether or not you are basically content with life without too many complications, or do you feel that a worthwhile life involves continuous growth and development?

Which attitude is better? I personally feel that the real definition of happiness is what I call continuous "creative dissatisfaction." Whatever the scores of the quizzes have shown, there should be room for working on yourself, striving ahead. This striving, in itself, is probably the best definition of the well-rounded and happy person.